EVERYDAY
PLAYS
for
BOYS AND GIRLS

by

HELEN LOUISE MILLER

Publishers   PLAYS, INC.   *Boston*

Library of Congress Cataloging-in-Publication Data

Gotwalt, Helen Louise Miller
  Everyday plays for boys and girls

  Summary: Fifteen one-act plays reflecting the interests of boys and girls in lower and middle grades.
  1. Children's plays, American. 2. One-act plays, American. [1. Plays] I. Title.
PS3513.075E84   1986   811'.52   86-8884
ISBN 0-8238-0274-4 (pbk.)

Contents

Circus Daze

Characters

CLANCY
VIC
SAM
ROY
ALF } *children*
SANDY
PATTY
MR. DARNUM, *circus owner*
LEON, *the lion tamer*
HUGO, *the human bullet*
SANCHO, *the sword swallower*
CARLOS, *of the Flying Crashendos*
GAUCHO THE GREAT, *the knife thrower*
MADAME COBRA, *the snake charmer*
MR. CUMMINGS, *Vic's father*

SETTING: *Outside a circus tent.*
BEFORE RISE: ROY, ALF, VIC, SAM, SANDY, *and* PATTY,
   all wearing jeans, enter. ROY *and* ALF *lie down at left*
   and peek under curtain; SANDY *and* PATTY *do the*

3

same at right. VIC *goes to center and peeks through opening of curtain. Offstage circus music is heard.*

SAM *(Trying to push* VIC *aside)*: Come on, Vic. You've looked long enough. It's my turn!

VIC: Not till the end of this act. Boy, Sam, you should see those elephants!

SAM: How can I see anything when you're hogging the best peephole? *(With a shove)* Come on! Move over! (CLANCY *enters left, unnoticed by others. He is dressed in old-fashioned police officer's costume and wears a false nose and moustache. He tiptoes center, and suddenly reaches out and grabs* VIC *and* SAM.)

CLANCY: Aha! Caught in the act! *(Other children scramble to feet.)* Stay right where you are! Don't move a muscle!

ALL *(Ad lib)*: Please! Please, Officer! Let us go! We haven't done anything! *(Etc.)*

VIC: We really didn't see much of the show. Honest!

CLANCY: You know it's against the law to sneak into a circus without a ticket.

SANDY: But we weren't sneaking, Officer. We were only peeking.

PATTY: If you let us go, we'll never do it again.

CLANCY: That's what they all say.

SAM: But we mean it!

CHILDREN: We promise!

VIC *(With air of importance)*: Besides, I have an uncle in this circus.

CLANCY *(Sarcastically)*: And who is this uncle of yours?

VIC *(Floundering)*: Well, sir, that's the tough part. I don't exactly know his name.

CLANCY: Ha! You don't know the name of your own uncle!

VIC: Well, you see, he's not *exactly* my uncle. He was a

friend of my dad's when they were boys, and he married a second cousin of my mother's aunt who lives in Peoria.

CLANCY (*Trying not to laugh*): And that's supposed to make him your uncle, is it?

VIC (*Doubtfully*): Well . . . yes, in a way.

CLANCY: A mighty funny sort of way, I'd call it. What is your name?

VIC: Victor—Victor Cummings the Third. And this is my friend, Sam Gallagher, and—

CLANCY: Hold on. You can all give your names at headquarters.

PATTY: I want to go home!

CLANCY: You'll go home soon enough, but first, you're coming with me.

ROY: Are you really taking us to Police Headquarters?

CLANCY: Who said anything about the police? I'm marching you right into Darnum and Daily Circus Headquarters. You can speak to Mr. Darnum himself. Now, get moving! (*He lines up children facing left and pushes them off ahead of him. As he turns to audience, he smiles broadly and waves. Curtains open.*)

* * *

SETTING: *Mr. Darnum's office. Several folding chairs and a table with circus props on it are at one side. Desk is center. Cardboard barbells labeled 2,000 LBS. are on floor.*

AT RISE: MR. DARNUM *sits at desk center.* ROY, ALF, VIC, SAM, SANDY, PATTY, *and* CLANCY *enter.*

MR. DARNUM (*Looking up, annoyed*): What's all this, Clancy? I gave strict orders I was not to be disturbed during show time.

CLANCY: An emergency, Mr. Darnum. I just caught

these young scamps trying to sneak in under the Big Top. I knew you would want to see them at once.

MR. DARNUM: Quite right. *(Turns to children)* Now, let's have your names *(Points to* SAM*)*, starting with you.

SAM: I'm Sam Gallagher, but we really weren't trying to sneak into the circus, sir. (MR. DARNUM *writes down name.)*

MR. DARNUM: When I want any explanations, I'll ask for them. Now, you. *(Points to* ROY*)* What's your name?

ROY: Roy—Roy Baker, Your Honor.

MR. DARNUM *(Writing):* You don't have to call me "Your Honor." This isn't a court of law. Next!

ALF: I'm Alf—Alfred Arthur Algernon Anderson. (MR. DARNUM *writes down name slowly, then looks at two girls.)*

MR. DARNUM: Now you two! I must say I'm surprised to see two girls mixed up in this!

SANDY: I'm Sandy Lou Davis.

PATTY: I'm Patricia Ann Evans.

CLANCY: Sit down—both of you. *(They sit.* CLANCY *points to* VIC.*)* This fellow seems to be the ringleader, Mr. Darnum. Calls himself Victor Cummings the Third and claims he has an uncle working with our show.

MR. DARNUM: Cummings, eh? Where do you live?

VIC: 918 Columbia Boulevard.

MR. DARNUM *(Writing):* This uncle of yours—what does he do in our circus?

VIC *(Uneasily):* Well, sir, I don't exactly know. We haven't heard from him in a long time.

CLANCY: And he says he isn't *exactly* his uncle either, and he doesn't *exactly* know his name.

VIC: But I do know that Dad always called him

"Sawdust," and that's how he used to sign the postcards he sent us.

CLANCY *and* MR. DARNUM: Sawdust!

CLANCY: There's nobody in this circus by that name.

SAM: We should have known Vic was only kidding us.

ALF: That's really why we came here . . . to meet Vic's uncle.

ROY: Vic said he might even give us a job with the circus.

MR. DARNUM: A job! You mean you kids really want to leave home and join the circus?

ALL: Sure! You bet!

MR. DARNUM: But what would your parents think?

ALF: Oh, they wouldn't mind . . . not after we become famous.

PATTY: And we'd let them know where we were so they wouldn't worry.

MR. DARNUM: Hm-m-m! (*To* CLANCY) Well, Clancy, if these boys and girls really want jobs, maybe we can put them to work. (*Writes and hands paper to* CLANCY) Clancy, follow these instructions. Several of our performers said they need assistants. As soon as they've finished their acts, bring them to my office. (*Writes again, hands folded sheet to* CLANCY) And then do what I've said here.

CLANCY: Very good, sir. (CLANCY *exits right.*)

MR. DARNUM (*Leaning back in his chair*): Now then, let's see what you can do. Do any of you have any experience in show business?

ROY: I did a tumbling act in our school circus.

MR. DARNUM: Fine! Let's have a demonstration.

ROY: You mean right now? Here?

MR. DARNUM: No time like the present. (ROY *does a few feeble somersaults and attempts a cartwheel unsuc-*

cessfully.) Hm-m-m. *(Makes a note)* What about you? *(Points to* ALF)

ALF: I've been practicing weight lifting in the gym.

MR. DARNUM: Good! *(Points to weight)* See what you can do with that. (ALF *tugs and heaves but can't budge it.*)

ALF *(Wiping his brow):* I do better with dumbbells and Indian clubs.

MR. DARNUM: I'll make a note of that. *(Points to* SAM) Now you! What can you do?

SAM: I have a book on juggling, but I've read only the first chapter.

MR. DARNUM *(Pointing to stack of plates on prop table):* Help yourself to those plates and give it a try.

SAM *(Attempting to juggle three plates and dropping all of them):* I guess I need more practice.

MR. DARNUM: Hm-m-m! I agree. Now we'll see what Victor Cummings the Third can do.

ROY: Show him your clown routine, Vic.

VIC: I—I'm afraid I don't feel very funny right now.

MR. DARNUM: A circus clown is funny whether he feels like it or not. Go ahead. Make me laugh.

VIC: O.K. I'll try. *(He does a few exaggerated steps, trips over his own feet and falls flat.)*

MR. DARNUM *(Writing):* Well, I'll give you credit for trying. Maybe you'd be funnier with a costume and make-up. Let's see if the girls have any circus talent. *(To* SANDY) Do you have any accomplishments?

SANDY: I've had some dancing lessons, but I don't know too many steps. *(Does a few ballet steps with a twirl or two)*

MR. DARNUM: Not bad! Do you think you could do some of those steps on a high wire . . . say, maybe fifty feet above the ground?

SANDY: Oh, no! I get dizzy on a low stepladder.

MR. DARNUM *(Writing):* O.K.! That's out. *(To* PATTY*)* That leaves you. What can you do?

PATTY: I do baton twirling, but I don't have my baton.

MR. DARNUM *(Indicating prop table):* There's one on the table. Help yourself. (PATTY *gets baton and does a short exhibition of baton twirling.)* You might have some possibilities. A lighted torch on either end of your baton would make your act more spectacular.

PATTY *(Frightened):* Oh, I couldn't. I'm scared to death of fire.

MR. DARNUM: Then that's out. Well, children, I must admit I have not been too impressed with your talent. But since I believe in giving young people a chance, we'll see if any of our performers can use you. (LEON, *the lion tamer, enters right. He wears a shirt which is badly ripped.)*

LEON: You sent for me, Mr. Darnum?

MR. DARNUM: Yes, Leon. I want you to meet some real circus fans. But perhaps you'd better see about those scratches first.

LEON: Oh, they're nothing, Mr. Darnum. The lions were a bit on the cranky side today—nothing to worry about.

MR. DARNUM: Boys and girls, this is Leon, our lion tamer. *(Children acknowledge introduction.)* Leon has been looking for someone to give him a hand with the big cats. *(Points to* ALF*)* This young man has been developing his muscles with weight lifting, Leon. I thought you might want to look him over.

LEON *(Inspecting* ALF*)*: Well, he does look like a strong boy, and I do need someone with strong shoulder muscles to work out that new wrestling act I've been planning with Tina the Tigress.

ALF *(Nervously):* I—I don't really think—I've never had

much experience with animals.

LEON: Oh, don't worry about that. Tina's still young and playful, and you could sort of grow up together. A few hours a day in her cage, and you might get along fine. On the other hand, if she didn't take a liking to you— well! You know how she acted with that last boy we tried, Mr. Darnum.

MR. DARNUM: You mean the one who's still in the hospital? He just wasn't her type. Now, this lad seems to have nerves of steel.

ALF *(Moving away):* Oh, no, sir, not really!

MR. DARNUM: What a pity. (HUGO *enters right. He wears a torn jacket and his face is badly smudged.)* Hugo! What happened to you?

HUGO: Something's wrong with that confounded cannon. This business of being shot out of a cannon twice a day is too much, Mr. Darnum. I just have to have an assistant.

MR. DARNUM: That's why I sent for you. Children, this is Hugo, the human bullet.

CHILDREN *(Ad lib):* Hi, hello. *(Etc.)*

MR. DARNUM *(Pointing to* ROY): This boy has been showing me some of his acrobatic stunts. Maybe you can use him in your act.

ROY: But I don't want to be shot out of a cannon.

HUGO *(Looking him over):* Not bad! And just about the right size. I like 'em young and limber.

ROY: My father always told me to stay away from guns.

HUGO: Oh, sure! Guns are dangerous, but a cannon . . . well, a cannon is different. You never need to worry about being *hit* by a bullet, when you *are* the bullet. Understand?

ROY: No, sir, I don't understand, and anyhow—

MR. DARNUM *(Looking off left):* Wait a minute. Someone

is in trouble. (SANCHO, *the sword swallower, enters left. He is dressed in Spanish costume, with a long cape that conceals a full-length sword in his belt. He has a sword handle in his mouth, and pretends to be struggling with it.*)

LEON: Sancho's sword is stuck again. Here, let me help. *(He crosses to* SANCHO *and turns him around so that* SANCHO's *back is to the audience. After a struggle,* LEON *pulls the sword from* SANCHO's *belt, making it appear as if he has pulled it from* SANCHO's *mouth.* SANCHO *conceals short handle under cape.)* There! Do you feel better, Sancho? (LEON *and* SANCHO *turn to face audience; children look at each other uneasily.*)

SANCHO *(Rubbing his throat):* Much better, thanks. But my throat still feels a little scratchy.

MR. DARNUM: Sancho, you're in luck. I think we've found you an assistant. *(Points to* SAM) This is Sam Gallagher. He wants to be a juggler, but I think he'd make a better sword swallower . . . with a little training.

SANCHO *(Clapping* SAM *on shoulder):* Good! You come with me, lad.

SAM *(Drawing back):* No! I don't want to swallow a sword!

SANCHO: Nonsense! I have a six-inch dagger that will do for a start. It's easy . . . much easier than fire-eating.

SAM: No! No! You let go of me! *(Pulls away)*

MR. DARNUM: Take it easy, Sancho. Give him a few minutes to get used to the idea. By the way, have you seen any of the Flying Crashendos?

SANCHO: I just passed Carlos on my way in here. Ah, here he is! (CARLOS *enters.*)

CARLOS: You sent for me?

MR. DARNUM: Yes, I want you to meet Vic Cummings—

Victor Cummings the Third. Vic, this is Carlos, one of the famous Flying Crashendos.

VIC: Hello, Mr. Carlos.

MR. DARNUM: Vic wants to be a clown, and you've been talking about adding some humor to your act.

CARLOS: A great idea! (*Looking at* VIC) He's just about the right weight, too, I think.

HUGO: How do you plan to use him?

CARLOS: When Marco and I are hanging by our heels from the two high bars, we can toss him back and forth between us.

VIC (*Excitedly*): Oh, no, you won't! Not me!

CARLOS: Every now and then we can miss the catch and Milo can grab him from the center trapeze ring. That should get a laugh. How about it, Vic?

VIC: Nothing doing! Let me out of here! (*He attempts to dash out right, but is stopped by* CLANCY *and* GAUCHO THE GREAT, *who are wheeling in a big sheet of cardboard with the outline of a girl on it.*)

MR. DARNUM: Aha! Here comes Gaucho the Great with something for the girls. (CLANCY *wheels the cardboard to center, facing audience.*)

GAUCHO: Your message came at the right moment, sir. My partner walked out on me without notice.

MR. DARNUM: I am quite sure that either one of these girls will be happy to work with Gaucho the Great, the most amazing knife thrower of all time.

CLANCY: We brought his equipment along, sir, so the girls can try it for size.

SANDY *and* PATTY (*Cringing; ad lib*): No! Not me! No way! (*Etc.*)

GAUCHO (*Taking* SANDY *by the hand*): This one will be perfect. (*Pulling her into place so that she is standing against the outline on the cardboard)* Look! A perfect fit!

SANDY *(Screaming):* No! Let go of me! Help!

GAUCHO: Don't be nervous, my child. I am Gaucho the Great. I never miss! Never! Not even when I am blindfolded.

PATTY: Why did your partner quit?

MR. DARNUM: Never ask awkward questions, child.

SANDY: I want to go home! *(Struggling)* Let go of me!

GAUCHO: Steady, steady, my dear. Your first lesson is not to wiggle—very important in knife-throwing. (MADAME COBRA *enters. Green snake is coiled around her neck. She carries a large covered reed basket.)*

MADAME COBRA: Sorry I'm late, Mr. Darnum, but I couldn't disappoint my public. What an audience! We took thirteen bows.

CHILDREN *(Screaming; ad lib):* A snake! Look out! A live snake! *(Etc.)*

MADAME COBRA: Of course it's a snake. What would you expect from a snake charmer? Now, do be quiet. You're disturbing Melinda. *(Stroking snake)* There, there, darling. These silly children won't hurt you. (*To* MR. DARNUM) You said you had an assistant for me. *(Pointing to* PATTY) Is that the one?

PATTY: No! Help! Let me out! (CLANCY *bars her way as she tries to run off, screaming.)*

CLANCY: Here, now! None of that!

MADAME COBRA: And stop that screaming! You're waking Cuddles, and he needs his rest. I can feel him stirring in his basket. *(As* PATTY *backs away)* Here! *(Offering basket to* PATTY) Take him and let him hear you sing. He likes anything slow and soothing.

PATTY (*Pulling away*): No! I won't touch it.

MADAME COBRA: This is an outrage, Mr. Darnum! This scamp is upsetting my pets!

MR. DARNUM (*To children*): Now, listen to me. I must say I am sadly disappointed in all of you. I've given you your chance to appear with some of the greatest stars of the Big Top, and you act like a bunch of scared rabbits. I now have no choice but to turn you over to the authorities. (MR. CUMMINGS *enters left. He goes to* MR. DARNUM *with outstretched hand.*)

MR. CUMMINGS: As I live and breathe, it's old Sawdust Dalrymple in the flesh! I came as soon as I got your message! How are you, you old rascal! (*They shake hands, and pound each other on the back.*)

MR. DARNUM: It's great to see you again, Victor.

VIC (*Running to his father*): Dad! Get us out of here!

PATTY: Please, Mr. Cummings, take us away!

MR. CUMMINGS (*As if surprised*): Vic! Sam! Patty! What are you doing here?

MR. DARNUM (*Laughing*): They're doing just what you and I did when we were kids, Victor. Clancy caught 'em trying to sneak in under the Big Top.

VIC: That's not so, Dad! We were only taking a peek.

CLANCY (*Shrugging*): Sneak or peek. It's all the same.

MR. DARNUM: Well, either way, it was a lucky thing. I've wanted to get in touch with you for years, Victor. I didn't even know you lived here till your boy gave me the tip. So I had Clancy give you a call.

MR. CUMMINGS: Too bad we lost track of each other, Sawdust. I had no idea the Darnum and Daily Circus belonged to you. When did you change your name?

MR. DARNUM: Years ago. "Dalrymple" was too long to fit on a circus poster.

MR. CUMMINGS: Vic, this is your Uncle Sawdust I've

been telling you about ever since you were a little boy.

VIC: Mr. Darnum, are you really my Uncle Sawdust?

MR. DARNUM: I sure am! When you said you were Victor Cummings the Third, I knew you were the son of my old friend.

ALF: Then why did you let that police officer arrest us?

CLANCY *(Taking off his false nose and moustache):* Arrest you? I'm no police officer. I'm just a circus clown, and this get-up is part of my act. I brought you in here because Mr. Darnum has such a soft heart for kids, he always likes to give them a real circus thrill.

SAM: He scared the living daylights out of us!

MR. DARNUM: I didn't really mean to scare you. But I do want to point out that running away to join a circus isn't always what it's cracked up to be.

LEON: You can tell all your friends at school that you've met some real circus stars.

HUGO: I'll be glad to give you my autograph.

SANCHO: And I'll let you in on some of my sword-swallowing secrets.

GAUCHO *(Bowing and kissing SANDY's hand):* I only regret that I cannot have such a charming lady as my partner.

MADAME COBRA: If you want to, I'll let you look at Cuddles. He's really sweet.

PATTY: No, thank you!

MR. CUMMINGS: It's been great to see you, Sawdust. When can we get together?

MR. DARNUM: Bring your family around to my tent after the show tonight. Clancy, give these children free passes for the next performance, enough for their whole class—the teacher, too!

ALL: Thanks, Mr. Darnum. That's great! *(They thank CLANCY as he distributes passes.)*

ROY: Now that I know I'm not going to be shot out of a cannon, this has been a great experience.

ALF: I can hardly wait to tell the rest of the kids that I met a real lion tamer.

SAM: And a sword swallower.

PATTY: And a snake charmer!

SANDY: They'll never believe us!

MR. CUMMINGS: They will, if you show them a picture. *(Takes camera out of his pocket)* I think we should have one for the record. This develops in ten seconds!

MR. DARNUM: Everyone get into the act. (MR. DARNUM *and* CLANCY *pose at center; performers pose with children.)* All set?

MR. CUMMINGS *(Looking into camera):* Come on now, relax! Smile! You all look as if you're in a daze!

VIC: You're right, Dad! We're in a real daze—a circus daze—and I don't think I ever want to wake up! (MR. CUMMINGS *snaps picture, as curtains close.)*

THE END

Bandit Ben Rides Again

Characters

WILD BILL
PEANUT BUTTER PETE } *cowboys*
JESSE JONES
SAD SAM
SHERIFF BUNCOMBE, *of Hokum County*
MIRANDA, *his daughter*
RED CHIEF
RED SQUAW
WHITE CHIEF
WHITE SQUAW
BLUE CHIEF
BLUE SQUAW
YELLOW CHIEF
YELLOW SQUAW
GREEN CHIEF
GREEN SQUAW
TILLY
MILLY } *city slickers*
WILLY
BANDIT BEN

TIME: *Just after the days of the wild West.*
SETTING: *Sheriff's office near the Bar-B.Q. Ranch.*

Crudely-lettered sign at the left reads BAR-B.Q.
RANCH; *another sign at right reads* SHERIFF'S OFFICE.
*There is a rail fence left, and right, a desk with swivel
chair. There is a large hand bell on desk.*

AT RISE: WILD BILL, PEANUT BUTTER PETE, JESSE
JONES, *and* SAD SAM *are perched on rail fence, idly
twirling their lassos.* SHERIFF BUNCOMBE *is slouched
in swivel chair, his hat pushed back on his head, feet
on desk; he is polishing his badge with bandanna.*

COWBOYS *(Singing to the tune of "Git Along, Little
Dogie"):*

> We're four little cowboys
> From Bar-B.Q. Ranch,
> We're four little cowboys
> Just waiting our chance
> To do something useful,
> To do something bold,
> Like real western heroes
> In brave days of old.

WILD BILL:

> We've counted our cattle,
> We've herded our sheep.

PEANUT BUTTER PETE:

> There's nothing to do
> But to eat and to sleep.

JESSE JONES:

> We're quick on the trigger,
> We're fast on the draw,

SAD SAM:

> We'd risk any danger
> Upholding the law.

ALL:

> But we've run out of robbers
> And bad men, you see,

'Cause all of them lately
Have jobs on TV!

SHERIFF *(Singing to tune of "Reuben, Reuben"):*
I'm the Sheriff of Hokum County
And I'm shining up my star,
'Cause it's getting kind of rusty
With affairs the way they are.

Why, there hasn't been a hold-up
Since I couldn't tell you when,
And the rustlers do not rustle
Since they're honest cattlemen.

So my star is getting rusty,
And my pistols are the same,
And my saddle's getting dusty,
Now the West is strictly tame!

WILD BILL: Well, boys, what shall we do this afternoon?

PEANUT BUTTER PETE: I'm going to make some fresh peanut butter sandwiches.

JESSE JONES: I'm going to write a letter.

SAD SAM: I'm going to read a sad, sad story, so I can have a good cry.

WILD BILL *(Yawning and stretching):* In that case, I might as well take a nap. *(As they prepare to exit; singing to the tune of "On Top of Old Smokey")*
It's back to the bunkhouse
For me and for you,
Because there's just nothing,
Just nothing to do!

(Cowboys exit.)

SHERIFF: I might as well go fishing. *(Calls off)* Oh, Miranda, will you please bring me my fishing rod and that can of worms in the shanty? (MIRANDA *enters with rod and bait can.)*

MIRANDA: Fishing again, Father?

SHERIFF: Why not? A man has to keep busy somehow. *(Picks up rod and bait can)*

MIRANDA: But we've had so much fish lately, I've started to sprout fins. I hope you don't catch any.

SHERIFF *(Sighing):* But I'm the Sheriff. If I can't catch outlaws, I might as well catch fish. *(Exits)*

MIRANDA *(Sitting in* SHERIFF's *chair):* Poor Father. He still misses the old days when there was a highwayman behind every bush. It certainly is quieter now. *(Five* CHIEFS *and five* SQUAWS *enter in single file. They wear costumes in colors of their names.* SQUAWS *carry camping equipment.* GREEN CHIEF *carries bows and arrows.)*

INDIANS *(Singing):*

> One little, two little, three little Indians,
> Four little, five little, six little Indians,
> Seven little, eight little, nine little Indians,
> Ten little Indians all!

RED CHIEF: This is a good place for camp. *(All set equipment down.)*

YELLOW CHIEF: Put the bows and arrows in a dry place, Green Chief.

GREEN CHIEF: Why bother? We never use them any more.

YELLOW CHIEF: They'll come in handy some day.

MIRANDA: Howdy, strangers.

INDIANS: Howdy.

MIRANDA: You aim to pitch camp here?

RED CHIEF: Yep.

MIRANDA: Good! Welcome to Hokum County. It's good to have some new neighbors.

RED CHIEF: You're here all alone? No men around?

MIRANDA: Only my father. He's the Sheriff. But he's out fishing right now.

WHITE CHIEF *(Pointing to Bar-B.Q. Ranch):* Who lives there?

MIRANDA: That's the Bar-B.Q. Ranch. The cowboys will also be glad to have new neighbors.

BLUE CHIEF: Is this a good place for camp?

MIRANDA: Oh, yes. *(Sighing)* Though nothing ever happens here. (TILLY, MILLY *and* WILLY *enter, screaming in terror.)*

TILLY: Help, help! Sheriff!

MILLY: Murder!

WILLY: Sheriff! Help!

BLUE CHIEF: What's wrong?

TILLY: Help! Murder!

MILLY: Help! Help!

MIRANDA: Stop that screaming and tell us what's wrong.

WILLY *(Breathlessly):* We've been robbed! We've been robbed!

MIRANDA: In Hokum County? Impossible! Who are you, anyway?

TILLY, MILLY *and* WILLY *(Reciting together):*
> We're three City Slickers,
> As green as can be.
> We don't know a cactus
> From a Joshua Tree!

TILLY: I'm Tilly!

MILLY: I'm Milly!

WILLY: I'm Willy!

MIRANDA: How did you get here? Where are your horses?

TILLY:
> We never ride horses,
> We're fresh from New York.
> Our stagecoach was held up
> At Red River Fork!

MIRANDA: How exciting!

MILLY (*Pointing at Indians; screaming in terror*): Indians! Indians! Help, help!

MIRANDA: Calm down. These Indians won't hurt you.

WILLY (*Trembling*): We'll never see home again.

MILLY (*Whimpering*): We'll be their captives for life.

TILLY (*Falling on her knees*): Spare, oh spare us, merciful Chief.

WHITE CHIEF (*Shaking head*): Too much sun can make you crazy.

YELLOW CHIEF (*Firmly*): This calls for a council. (*To* TILLY) Sit down. Tell us your story. (*Indians sit in semicircle, while* TILLY, MILLY, *and* WILLY *stand center.* MIRANDA *goes to desk.*)

MIRANDA: Now, tell us what really happened to you.

TILLY: It was just the way we told you.

MILLY: Our stage was held up at Red River Fork . . .

WILLY: By a big bandit wearing a black mask.

TILLY: He took all of my bracelets.

MILLY: And all of my rings.

WILLY: And all of our money.

GREEN CHIEF: What happened to the stagecoach driver?

TILLY: The horses ran off with the coach and driver.

MIRANDA: I'll call my father. He'll know what to do. This is our alarm bell. (*Rings bell*) We always ring it in times of trouble. (*Rings bell louder*) It will also rouse the boys at Bar-B.Q. Ranch. We haven't had so much excitement in years. (*Cowboys run in left.* PEANUT BUTTER PETE *is munching on a sandwich.*)

JESSE JONES: What's up?

MIRANDA: Plenty. A bandit just held up the stage at Red River Fork. These people were robbed.

WILD BILL: Come on, men. We'd better see if the cattle are all right.

SAM: Let's go! Pete, finish up that sandwich, and we'll saddle the horses. (*Cowboys exit.*)

RED CHIEF (*To* RED SQUAW): Get the bows and arrows.

GREEN CHIEF (*To* GREEN SQUAW): Bring the war paint, too.

MIRANDA *(Objecting):* You don't need war paint to catch a bandit.

GREEN SQUAW: War paint is good medicine. It scares bandits.

SHERIFF *(Entering with rod and pail):* Miranda, what in tarnation is going on here? You scared me to death ringing that bell, and besides, my biggest fish got away.

MIRANDA: Father, I'm glad you're here!

TILLY: Our stage was held up at Red River Fork.

MILLY: And the bandit took all our money and jewelry.

WILLY: You must catch him at once.

SHERIFF: That we'll do. (*Pompously*) Sheriff Buncombe always gets his man. I'll get up a posse right away.

WHITE CHIEF: Indian neighbors ready to ride with paleface.

SHERIFF (*To* MIRANDA): Where did these Indians come from?

MIRANDA: They're our new neighbors, Father. They're very friendly.

SHERIFF *(To Indians):* Then get your horses at once. (CHIEFS *exit.*) Did you see which way the bandit went?

TILLY, MILLY *and* WILLY *(Pointing):* He went that-a-way!

SHERIFF: Did you call the boys from Bar-B.Q. Ranch?

MIRANDA: They've gone to see their cattle and saddle their horses.

SHERIFF: Good. I'll saddle Old Paint and be ready to ride. (*Exits. Cowboys enter on broomstick horses.*)

WILD BILL: That miserable bandit stole some of our best cattle.

JESSE JONES: We'll hang that varmint on a sour apple tree. (*Indians enter on broomstick horses.*)

MIRANDA: Our new Indian neighbors are joining the posse.

WILD BILL: Good.

SHERIFF (*Entering on broomstick horse*): No doubt the villain is hiding in Cabbage Canyon. We'll cut him off at Snake Tooth Gap.

WILLY: Maybe I'd better go with you.

SHERIFF: No, you stay here with the ladies. (*To Cowboys*) Come on, fellows, let's go. (*Cowboys and Indians circle stage once, shouting and yelling, then exit left.*)

MIRANDA: I wish I could go along.

YELLOW SQUAW: No place for women. We'll stay and set up the camp.

MIRANDA (*To TILLY, MILLY and WILLY*): Make yourselves at home. (SQUAWS *busy themselves with camp equipment.*) I'll help the squaws. (*She joins* SQUAWS. MILLY, TILLY, *and* WILLY *sit on floor as* BANDIT BEN *enters, wearing a black half-mask. He carries a bag of loot in one hand and brandishes toy pistol in the other.*)

BANDIT: Stick 'em up. (SQUAWS *and* MIRANDA *turn in surprise.* MILLY, TILLY, *and* WILLY *jump to their feet.*)

ALL (*Ad lib*): The bandit! The bandit! He'll kill us! Help! Help! (*Etc.*)

BANDIT (*Pointing pistol*): Reach for the sky! (*All raise their hands.*) Now . . . (*Looks around*) nobody here but the ladies, I see. Where are the men?

WILLY: I'm right here. And if you think I'm afraid of that gun, you . . . *(Stammering)* you're right.

MIRANDA *(To* BANDIT*)*: What's your name? And what do you think you're doing here?

BANDIT *(Removing mask; staggering as he recites):*
I'm a big, bad bandit, by the name of Ben.
I'm a rootin', tootin' rascal from El Gaucho Glen!
All the cowboys tremble, and their horses shy,
And the Injuns quake and quiver when I just ride by!
I'm a big, bold, bad man from the wild, wild West,
And of all the old-time outlaws, I'm the last and the best!
I'm a big, bad bandit, as bad as I can be,
And it does no good to chase me, 'cause you can't catch me!

MIRANDA *(Defiantly):* Well, my father will catch you. He's out looking for you right now.

BANDIT: A lot of good it will do him. I knew he'd go that-a-way *(Pointing)*, so I came this-a-way.

MILLY *and* TILLY: Help! Help!

BANDIT: Stop that screeching. I never did like a screaming woman. Be quiet, and you won't be hurt.

MIRANDA: What do you want?

BANDIT: First of all, I want something to eat. Have any pie?

MIRANDA: I—I think so.

BANDIT: Bring me a nice big piece. And while you're at it, fry some potatoes and cook a steak. I like it rare and juicy.

MIRANDA: I'm not the cook here.

BANDIT: Don't put on airs. *(Brandishing gun)* Get into the house and do as I say.

MIRANDA: But I'm really *not* the cook. Grub Smith cooks

at our house, and he's a good one, too.

BANDIT: Then tell Grub Smith to get moving and bring me some good food. I'm starving.

MIRANDA: He—he's not here right now. He's out in the barn. *(Starting left)* I'll go get him.

BANDIT: No tricks, little lady. You stay right here where I can keep my eyes on you.

MIRANDA: Oh, I don't need to go to the barn. I can call him with this bell. He'll come running the minute he hears it.

BANDIT: O.K., then. Go ahead and ring it, and make it plenty loud. *(Hands to stomach)* I'm as hungry as a grizzly bear.

MIRANDA *(Ringing violently, then pausing):* I guess he's inside the barn. Maybe he can't hear me. I'll ring again. *(Rings louder and louder. As she rings,* SHER-IFF, *Cowboys and Indians gallop back onstage on broomstick horses.)*

COWBOYS *and* INDIANS *(Ad lib):* The bandit! The bandit! He's here! Nab him! *(Etc.)*

SHERIFF: Tie him up. *(Cowboys and Indians disarm* BANDIT. WILD BILL *ties him up.)* I told you Sheriff Buncombe always gets his man. Now, what shall we do with him?

SAD SAM: String him up.

PEANUT BUTTER PETE: Ride him out on a rail.

JESSE JONES: Tar and feather him.

WILD BILL: That's too good for him.

MIRANDA: Easy, boys—easy. We must give him a fair trial.

RED CHIEF: Make him run the gauntlet.

SAD SAM: That's not a bad idea.

MIRANDA: Father, we can't do that. As a lawman, you must stand for law and order.

SHERIFF: But this man is a dangerous character, daughter.

WILLY: I have an idea, Sheriff.

SHERIFF: We don't need any of your big city ideas. We have our own laws here in the West.

WILLY: But this is a great idea, sir.

SHERIFF: O.K., let's hear it.

WILLY: I want you to turn him over to me.

SHERIFF: What for? What would you do with him?

WILLY (*Producing card and handing it to* SHERIFF): Sir, my card.

SHERIFF (*Reading*): Willy Winkum, President of Terror, Incorporated.

WILLY: If you turn him over to me, Sheriff, I'll put him on television and keep him there for the rest of his life.

BANDIT (*Pleading*): Oh, please, no, Sheriff. Anything but that.

TILLY: The last of the Bad Men!

BANDIT: I don't want to be a Bad Man on television. The Bad Men never win. The bandits are always caught.

SHERIFF: Well, you're caught now, and it's up to us to decide. All those in favor of putting this wretch on television say "aye"!

ALL: Aye!

SHERIFF: So be it. Mr. Winkum, he's your prisoner. Take him away. (*Pushes* BANDIT *toward* WILLY, *who takes him by his arm*)

WILLY: I promise you he will never escape. He will be caught and punished on every T.V. show.

ALL: Hurray! Hurray!

WILD BILL:

> And now my little friends
> When you're watching T.V.

JESSE JONES:

> Just think how unhappy
> This bandit will be!

PEANUT BUTTER PETE:

> No matter how quick,
> The hero is quicker!

SAD SAM:

> No matter how slick,
> The good guys are slicker!

SHERIFF:

> And not once, but always,
> Again and again,
> They'll capture the bandit,
> And that will be Ben!

MIRANDA:

> 'Twill be a lot safer
> For you and for me,
> To keep this bold bandit
> For life on T.V.! *(Curtain)*

THE END

So Long at the Fair

Characters

JOHNNY ARMSTRONG
BETSY ARMSTRONG, *his sister*
PATTY WEBSTER
MRS. WEBSTER, *her mother*
BILLY
PEGGY
BOBBY
POLICE OFFICER
FOUR BARKERS
CAROUSEL ATTENDANT
GYPSY
CHILDREN, *extras*

SCENE 1

TIME: *The present.*
SETTING: *Bus stop. May be played before curtain. Sign at right reads* BUS STOP. *There are two benches at rear.*
AT RISE: MRS. WEBSTER, BETSY, PATTY, BILLY, BOBBY, *and* PEGGY *stand near or sit on benches, holding stuffed animals, balloons, and other souvenirs.*

BETSY *(Passing balloon to* PATTY*):* Patty, would you hold this for me while I take my shoes off? My feet are killing me.

PATTY: We must have walked miles today.

BOBBY: I'm hungry!

BILLY: Me, too! I could eat a horse.

MRS. WEBSTER: But, boys, you've done nothing but eat all day.

BOBBY: Only three hamburgers, two hot dogs, an ice cream cone, and two sodas.

PATTY: I wish Johnny would hurry up so we can go home.

MRS. WEBSTER: I can't imagine where he is. I'm beginning to get worried.

ALL *(Singing to the tune of "Oh dear! What Can the Matter Be?"):*
> "Oh, dear! What can the matter be?
> Dear, dear! What can the matter be?
> Oh, dear! What can the matter be?
> Johnny's so long at the fair."

BOBBY: The last time I saw him he was getting off the merry-go-round.

PATTY: The last time I saw him he was eating a hot dog.

PEGGY: The last time I saw him he was riding the Ferris wheel.

MRS. WEBSTER: When was the last time you saw him, Betsy?

BETSY *(Slowly):* I don't know. . . . He went off looking for something.

MRS. WEBSTER: Looking for something? Do you know *what*?

BETSY: I . . . I think he was looking for a present. . . . for me.

MRS. WEBSTER: A present for you?

BETSY *(Singing to the tune of "Oh dear! What Can the Matter Be?"):*
"He promised he'd buy me a fairing should please me,
And then for a kiss,
Oh, he vowed he would tease me,
He promised he'd buy me a bunch of blue ribbons,
To tie up my bonnie brown hair."
ALL:
"Oh, dear! What can the matter be?
Dear, dear! What can the matter be?
Oh, dear! What can the matter be?
Johnny's so long at the fair."
MRS. WEBSTER: I do hope he isn't lost.
BILLY: Johnny couldn't get lost on this fairground. He knows every inch of it. (POLICE OFFICER *enters left and strolls across stage.)*
PEGGY: Here comes a policeman. Maybe he can help us.
MRS. WEBSTER *(To* POLICE OFFICER): Good afternoon, Officer. Have you seen a boy *(Gesturing)* about so high, wearing blue jeans and a red sweater?
POLICE OFFICER: I've seen a dozen boys who would fit that description, ma'am. *(Pulls out notebook)* What's his name?
BETSY: Johnny—Johnny Armstrong. He's my brother.
MRS. WEBSTER: I'm afraid he's lost.
POLICE OFFICER: I'll take a look around the grounds and see if I can find him.
MRS. WEBSTER: Maybe we should go with you.
POLICE OFFICER: No need for that, ma'am. Why don't you wait in the bus station? I'll bring the boy here the minute I find him.
MRS. WEBSTER: Thank you. We're all tired. Come along, children. *(All except* POLICE OFFICER *exit right.)*
POLICE OFFICER *(Reading from notebook):* Johnny

Armstrong. Blue jeans, red sweater. Hm-m-m. This will be like looking for a needle in a haystack, but I'll find him! *(Exits left. Curtain)*

*****

SCENE 2

SETTING: *Fairgrounds. There are four brightly-colored booths.*

AT RISE: CHILDREN *are playing make-believe "Carousel," walking in two circles, one inside the other. (See Production Notes.)* CAROUSEL ATTENDANT *stands beside merry-go-round.* BARKERS *stand behind each booth.*

CHILDREN *(Singing to the tune of "Carousel"):*
"Little children, sweet and gay,
Carousel is running.
It will run till evening.
Little ones a nickel, big ones a dime.
Hurry up, get your mate,
Or you'll surely be too late.
Ha, ha, ha, happy are we, Peterson and Henderson and Anderson and me!
Ha, ha, ha, happy are we, Peterson and Henderson and Anderson and me!"

CAROUSEL ATTENDANT: Everybody off! End of the ride! Line up for tickets. Little ones a nickel, big ones a dime. *(Children break up carousel formation. A few scatter to the four booths. Others buy tickets and form smaller circles for next game, which they play silently.* JOHNNY, *who is one of the carousel players, approaches* CAROUSEL ATTENDANT. JOHNNY *carries a straw hat and some blue ribbons.)*

JOHNNY: Please, mister, may I have a fairing?

ATTENDANT: A fairing? Don't you mean a ticket?

JOHNNY: No, sir, a fairing. I promised my sister I'd bring her one.

ATTENDANT: Well, I've never heard of such a thing. What is it?

JOHNNY: I got the idea from a song we sing at school. I'm sure you get them at fairs.

ATTENDANT *(Shaking head; pointing to booth at right):* Why don't you try over there?

JOHNNY: Thanks, I will. *(Walks to first booth at right)*

1ST BARKER: Right this way for the best buys at the fair!

JOHNNY *(To* 1ST BARKER*):* Say, mister, do you have any fairings?

1ST BARKER: Any what?

JOHNNY: Fairings. I'd like to buy one.

1ST BARKER: Fairings, eh? Never heard of them, boy. *(Reciting or singing to tune of "Oh dear! What Can the Matter Be?")*

> I've hot dogs and burgers
> With mustard and pickles,
> For only some change
> Or five dimes and four nickels.
> I've custard and ice cream
> In forty-two flavors,
> But nary a fairing have I.

JOHNNY *(Sighing):* It's getting late, and I must find a fairing before I leave. *(Moving right)* I'll try the next booth.

2ND BARKER: Hurry, hurry, hurry! Get 'em while they're hot. *(Noticing* JOHNNY*)* What can I do for you, young fellow?

JOHNNY: I'd like to buy a fairing, sir.

2ND BARKER: A fairing, eh? Never heard of that, boy.

(Reciting or singing to tune of "Oh dear! What Can the Matter Be?")

> I've popcorn and peanuts,
> And real cotton candy.
> I've lemonade, soda,
> And popsicles handy.
> I've ginger ale, root beer,
> Right here in the cooler,
> But nary a fairing have I.

1ST CHILD: Did I hear you ask for a fairing?

JOHNNY: Yes. Do you know where I can get one?

1ST CHILD *(Pointing left):* Right over there. That man has all sorts of pretty things.

JOHNNY: Thanks, thanks a lot. *(Moves to next booth)*

3RD BARKER: Here's what you've been waiting for. Something for everyone—right this way!

JOHNNY: How much are your fairings, mister?

3RD BARKER: My what?

JOHNNY: Your fairings. I'd like to buy one.

3RD BARKER: Sorry, young man. I've none of those. *(Reciting or singing to tune of "Oh dear! What Can the Matter Be?")*

> I've rings for your fingers,
> And bracelets and lockets.
> I've bright-colored aprons
> With pretty patch pockets.
> I've real leather wallets
> To carry your money,
> But nary a fairing have I.

JOHNNY *(Worried):* What am I going to do? I'll try one more booth. *(Goes to last booth)*

4TH BARKER: Right this way, friends. Step right up for the cuddliest toys in the world. *(To JOHNNY)* Hello, there. How would you like this fine teddy bear?

JOHNNY: No thanks, mister. I'm looking for a fairing.

4TH BARKER: Sorry, we just sold our last one, my friend. *(Singing to tune of "Oh dear! What Can the Matter Be?")*

> I've teddy bears, pandas,
> And dolls dressed in laces,
> And poppets and puppets
> With Mickey Mouse faces.
> And here's Donald Duck
> And a real alligator,
> But nary a fairing have I.

JOHNNY *(Discouraged):* Well, I guess I'll have to go home without one. *(As he turns to cross right, he comes face to face with GYPSY, who is entering.)*

GYPSY: Not so fast, my pretty gentleman. You can't leave without hearing your fortune.

JOHNNY: I don't want to hear my fortune. I want to go home.

GYPSY *(Holding hands to the side of JOHNNY's head):* Ah, there is an air of trouble about you. . . . You are in some kind of trouble.

JOHNNY: How . . . how did you know?

GYPSY: Ah, that is my secret. Just cross my palm with silver and I'll tell you what is troubling you.

JOHNNY: I already know what's troubling me. I promised my sister I'd buy her a fairing, and I can't find a single one.

GYPSY: So that is it! Well, as it just so happens, my young friend, I can help you.

JOHNNY: How?

GYPSY *(Extending her hand):* First, I must see your silver.

JOHNNY: But this is my last coin. If I give it to you, I won't have any money left to buy a fairing.

GYPSY: Without hearing my fortune, you will know of no fairings to buy.

JOHNNY *(Slowly)*: Oh, all right. *(Pulls coin from pocket and hands it to her)*

GYPSY *(Smiling)*: Ah, good, Now, let me see your hand. (JOHNNY *holds out hand, and* GYPSY *pretends to read it.* POLICE OFFICER *enters left.*)

POLICE OFFICER *(Noticing them)*: Here, here! What's going on? *(To* GYPSY*)* I've told you fortunetelling is forbidden on this fairground.

JOHNNY: She isn't telling my fortune, Officer. She's helping me find a fairing. I promised my sister I'd get her one.

POLICE OFFICER: A fairing? What does a gypsy fortuneteller know about fairings?

GYPSY *(Proudly)*: More than you think, Officer. I happen to have the very thing this young gentleman is looking for. *(Pulls small charm on a silver chain from her pocket)* Here, lad, you shall have your fairing.

JOHNNY *(In wonder)*: Is this *really* a fairing?

GYPSY: It is a good luck charm my grandfather gave me many years ago.

JOHNNY: Oh, thank you, thank you! I am sure my sister will love it.

GYPSY *(Bowing)*: May it bring you both the best of luck.

JOHNNY: I'm sure it will.

GYPSY: So you see, Officer, I wasn't telling fortunes. I was just making an honest sale.

POLICE OFFICER *(Shaking his head)*: I'll let you go this time, but don't let me catch you around here again.

GYPSY *(Earnestly)*: No, sir! *(As she exits)* Not if I see you first, Officer!

JOHNNY *(Examining trinket)*: Is this really a fairing, Officer?

POLICE OFFICER (*Putting hand on* JOHNNY's *shoulder*): You could call it that. A fairing is just a trinket. . . . a souvenir.

JOHNNY: It is? Wow! If I'd known that, I could have bought anything in one of those booths. (*Pausing*) I guess I never really knew what the word meant.

POLICE OFFICER (*Taking a closer look at* JOHNNY): Say, does your name (*Pulls out notebook*) happen to be Johnny Armstrong?

JOHNNY (*Puzzled*): Yes, that's me. But how did you know?

POLICE OFFICER: You've only kept half a dozen people waiting. They think you're lost, and they've sent me out to look for you. (*Placing hand on* JOHNNY's *shoulder*) Don't you know you should never wander off by yourself?

JOHNNY: I'm sorry, sir. I guess I didn't think. I'll go find them right away. (MRS. WEBSTER *enters from right with* BETSY, PATTY, PEGGY, BILLY, *and* BOBBY.)

BETSY (*Running to* JOHNNY): There he is! There's Johnny!

MRS. WEBSTER: Oh, thank goodness, Officer, you've found him.

BETSY: Oh, Johnny, you have my hat and ribbons.

JOHNNY (*Handing her the charm*): And here's your fairing. I hope you like it.

BETSY: It's beautiful!

PATTY: Where did you find it?

JOHNNY: It's a long story. I'll tell you about it on the way home.

MRS. WEBSTER: Where have you been, Johnny? What kept you?

JOHNNY: I was trying to find the fairing I promised Betsy.

MRS. WEBSTER: A fairing? What's that, Johnny?

PATTY: We sing a song about it in school, Mother. It goes like this.

ALL *(Singing):*

> Oh, dear! What can the matter be?
> Dear, dear! What can the matter be?
> Oh, dear! What can the matter be?
> Johnny's so long at the fair.

BETSY: He promised to buy me a fairing to please me. . . .

JOHNNY: See! That's where I got the idea!

POLICE OFFICER (*To* MRS. WEBSTER): "Fairing" is an old English word for trinket or souvenir. Not many people use it any more.

PEGGY: The word trinket fits the music just as well.

BETTY: Well, *I* like fairing, and if Johnny went to all the trouble to get me one, I'm going to keep right on singing the song the way we learned it.

BOBBY: At least now we understand why Johnny was so long at the fair! (*All exit singing "Oh dear! What Can the Matter Be?" as curtain falls.*)

THE END

Sourdough Sally

Characters

SALLY CRANE
MRS. CRANE, *her mother*
DAISY ⎱ *her friends*
EDITH ⎰
BLACKBEARD ⎫
GRAYBEAD ⎪
BROWNBEARD ⎬ *prospectors*
YELLOWBEARD ⎪
REDBEARD ⎭
THORA ⎱ *Aleut twins*
KOOTUK ⎰
SOURDOUGH CHARLIE
MS. COLLINS, *teacher*

TIME: *The present. A spring day.*
SETTING: *The Crane living room in Alaska. Large easel with painting of Alaskan flag is located at center. The flag has eight gold stars on a blue field, arranged to represent the Big Dipper and the North Star. One door leads outside, another to the rest of house.*
AT RISE: SALLY CRANE *is painting at easel.* MRS. CRANE *stands near her, observing painting.*

MRS. CRANE: That's a fine flag, Sally. Every star is perfect, and the Dipper is just right.

SALLY *(Happily):* It's such a beautiful flag and so right for Alaska, the land of the North Star.

MRS. CRANE *(Laughing):* I still remember how homesick you were when we first came to Alaska. Now you're a regular little sourdough.

SALLY: Not a real sourdough. To my friends at school, I'm still a *Chee-cha-ko,* a newcomer. *(Sighing)* Oh, I hope I'll get the part of Miss Alaska in the school play, so I can recite the poem about the flag. I know every word of it.

MRS. CRANE: You have as good a chance as anyone else.

SALLY: But they are choosing the parts today, and I've been absent a whole week. We're having the play to celebrate the spring break-up.

MRS. CRANE: You even talk like a sourdough. A year ago you weren't the least bit interested in the ice breaking up.

SALLY: Now that I've lived through an Alaskan winter, I know spring is something to celebrate. *(Doorbell rings.)*

MRS. CRANE *(As she crosses to door):* We should also celebrate the fact that you're finally over that nasty cold! *(Opens door to* DAISY, EDITH, *and* THORA*)* Hi, girls. Come on in. Sally will be glad to see you.

GIRLS *(Ad lib):* Hi, Mrs. Crane. Thanks. *(Etc. They cross to* SALLY, *ad lib greetings.)* Hi, Sally. How do you feel? We've missed you. *(Etc.)*

SALLY: Oh, I feel fine now. I'm glad you're all here. I'm dying to hear all the news from school!

MRS. CRANE: Sally's been pretty lonely for the last week. *(Looks at watch)* You girls have a good time. I have to run out for a little while to do some errands. I'll be back soon.

GIRLS *(Ad lib):* Bye. See you later. *(Etc.* MRS. CRANE *exits.)*

EDITH *(Seeing flag):* Look—the Alaskan flag!

THORA *(Inspecting it):* It's beautiful. Ms. Collins should see this.

DAISY: Who's the artist?

SALLY *(Shyly):* I am. Do you think it's good enough to use in our spring program?

EDITH *(Enthusiastically):* It's perfect.

SALLY: Thanks, Edith. . . . Now for the news. Did you all get parts in the play?

DAISY: I'm one of the Indian dancers.

SALLY: Good for you, Daisy!

EDITH: I'm in the chorus, but Thora and her brother Kootuk have speaking parts.

SALLY *(To* THORA*):* Great! You must be thrilled.

THORA: I am, but Kootuk wanted to be a soldier. Since he and I are the only Aleuts in the class, Ms. Collins wants us to play the parts of Aleut twins and tell about some of our customs.

DAISY: And they're going to bring Seego, the sled dog. *(Doorbell rings.)*

THORA: I hope that's Kootuk with the rest of the boys.

SALLY: Boys?

EDITH: Yes—they have a surprise for you. I'll let them in. (EDITH *crosses to door;* KOOTUK *enters, walks to center.)*

KOOTUK: Hi, Sally. You don't look sick to me.

SALLY: Hi, Kootuk. Thanks. I feel much better.

THORA: Where are the others, Kootuk?

KOOTUK: They stopped at the Trading Post. Mr. Smith

has a real, live grizzly down there, and they wanted to see it. *(Doorbell rings.)* That's probably the rest of the gang now. Wait till you see them! (KOOTUK *crosses to door, admits six boys.* REDBEARD, BLACKBEARD, GRAYBEARD, BROWNBEARD, *and* YELLOWBEARD *wear jeans, appropriately colored beards, and carry spades over their shoulders.* SOURDOUGH CHARLIE *carries a pie pan. They march on, singing to the tune of "Clementine," and form a semicircle around* SOURDOUGH CHARLIE.)

BOYS *(Singing):*
> In Alaska, in Alaska,
> In the land of ice and snow,
> Lived a miner, ninety-niner,
> Making bread with sourdough.

> Sourdough Charlie, Sourdough Charlie,
> Sourdough Charlie won us fame.
> Though he's lost and gone forever,
> True Alaskans bear his name.

ALL: Meet Sourdough Charlie, the star of our show!

SOURDOUGH CHARLIE *(With a bow):* Howdy, Sally! Glad you're well again!

SALLY: Thank you! So am I!

EDITH: How do you like their costumes?

THORA: And their song?

DAISY: And their beards?

SALLY: It's all great. And I love the beards, but why the different colors?

BLACKBEARD: So you can tell us apart. We are all prospectors from the Gold Rush. I'm Blackbeard.

BROWNBEARD: I'm Brownbeard. I tell how gold was discovered in Alaska.

YELLOWBEARD: I'm Yellowbeard. I wanted to get rich so badly that even my beard turned to gold.

GRAYBEARD: I'm Graybeard, an old-timer. I carry the sourdough pot and explain how the prospectors baked their bread from the yeast they always carried in their packs.

REDBEARD: I'm Redbeard. I explain why true Alaskans are called sourdoughs to this very day.

SOURDOUGH CHARLIE: And I'm Sourdough Charlie, the guy who struck it rich!

BOYS (Singing to the tune of "Clementine"):
    In the Yukon, in the Yukon,
    Where the men all searched for gold,
    Sourdough Charlie made a fortune,
    So the story has been told.

    Sourdough Charlie, Sourdough Charlie,
    Sourdough Charlie won us fame.
    Though he's lost and gone forever,
    True Alaskans bear his name.
    (Girls applaud.)

DAISY: I'm so glad you're coming back to school this week, Sally.

THORA: We have to rehearse every day.

SALLY (Wistfully): Are all the parts given out?

EDITH: Most of the speaking parts.

SALLY: Who is Miss Alaska?

KOOTUK: Ms. Collins hasn't decided yet.

SALLY: Do you think I have a chance?

EDITH: You are a good speaker, Sally, but . . . (Hesitating) you haven't been here very long.

KOOTUK: You're still a *Chee-cha-ko.*

SALLY (Upset): I am not! I am not a *Chee-cha-ko!* We've lived here almost a year, and I don't *feel* like a *Chee-cha-ko!*

THORA: But you're not a sourdough.

SALLY: That's not fair! Alaska is my state, even if I wasn't born here.

BLACKBEARD: None of us was born here except Thora and Kootuk.

GRAYBEARD: I just moved here three years ago.

SALLY: Then how come you're a sourdough, and I'm not?

SOURDOUGH CHARLIE: Did you ever throw a stone in the Yukon?

SALLY: Sure I did, lots of times.

YELLOWBEARD: Did you ever rub noses with an Eskimo?

SALLY: What's that got to do with being a sourdough?

REDBEARD: Everybody knows you have to throw a stone in the Yukon, rub noses with an Eskimo, and pet a grizzly bear before you can become a sourdough.

SALLY: That's easy. Come on, Thora, let's rub noses.

THORA: Eskimos don't rub noses any more, Sally. We've outgrown that silly custom.

SALLY: Well, can't you do it with me, just this once?

THORA: O.K., but I feel foolish! *(They rub noses.)*

SALLY: There! That makes me two-thirds of a sourdough right now.

KOOTUK: But you still have to pat a grizzly, and I wouldn't advise you to try that!

SALLY *(Almost in tears):* But I want to be a sourdough more than anything else in the world.

DAISY: Nobody pays any attention to that any more, Sally.

SALLY: But I want a chance to be Miss Alaska and recite the poem about the Alaskan flag.

THORA: There are plenty of other parts.

BLACKBEARD: Somebody has to tell about the history of Alaska.

GRAYBEARD: How it was purchased by Secretary of

State Seward from Russia in 1867.

YELLOWBEARD: And how everybody made fun of it and called Alaska "Seward's Folly" and "America's Ice Box."

SALLY: I hope I can get one part anyway. . . . Listen, I'll get us some cookies. I know Mother baked some this morning.

SOURDOUGH CHARLIE: Good! I never could work on an empty stomach, and I need to go over my welcome speech.

SALLY: Go right ahead. *(Exits)*

EDITH: Remember, none of you let on to Sally about the secret. *(To* CHARLIE*)* All right, Charlie. Let's hear your speech.

SOURDOUGH CHARLIE *(Clearing his throat):* O.K. Here goes. *(He walks center.)*

> Howdy folks!
> And welcome be ye
> To the forty-ninth state
> In the land of the free.
>
> 'Tis a great land, Alaska,
> And double in size
> The big state of Texas,
> The Westerners' prize.
>
> Our winters are long,
> And our summers are short,
> But here we have fishing
> And every great sport.
>
> Our riches are many,
> Our wealth is untold,
> And people still come here
> A-searching for gold.

> Alaskans are brave,
> And loyal and true,
> In fact you will find us
> Exactly like you!

(Applause)

KOOTUK: And now for the statehood poem. Let's all say it together.

ALL:

> In nineteen hundred fifty-eight,
> July the seventh was the date—
> A new state joined your land and mine:
> Alaska, number forty-nine!

(MRS. CRANE *enters with* MS. COLLINS.)

MS. COLLINS *(Clapping):* Bravo! Bravo!

THORA *(Surprised):* Ms. Collins! How did you get here?

MRS. CRANE: I met her in town, and she says she has a special surprise for Sally. Where is Sally, by the way?

DAISY: She just went out to the kitchen, to get some cookies.

MRS. CRANE: Good. I'll go fix some lemonade. *(Exits)*

MS. COLLINS: I hope none of you told Sally our secret.

KOOTUK: Wild horses wouldn't get it out of us.

MS. COLLINS: I can hardly wait to see her face.

EDITH: Look at the picture of the Alaskan flag Sally painted.

MS. COLLINS *(At easel):* It's lovely, and just what we need for the program. (MRS. CRANE *re-enters.*)

MRS. CRANE *(Upset):* Sally's not in the kitchen. Where could she be? Her coat isn't in the closet, but I know she wouldn't just leave when she has company.

THORA: You don't suppose—

MRS. CRANE: Suppose what? Do you know where Sally went?

THORA: Well, no, but—

KOOTUK: I think I know. You see, we were all teasing Sally about being a *Che-cha-ko,* and some of the boys were telling her that old legend about what you have to do to be a sourdough.

MRS. CRANE: What do you mean?

SOURDOUGH CHARLIE: Oh, it's all pretty silly, Mrs. Crane. There's an old saying that if you want to be a true sourdough, you have to throw a stone in the Yukon, rub noses with an Eskimo, and—and—pet a grizzly.

MRS. CRANE: Pet a grizzly! Thank goodness there are no grizzlies around here, or she just might be foolish enough to try.

SOURDOUGH CHARLIE *(Uneasily):* That's the trouble, Mrs. Crane. There is a grizzly down at the Trading Post.

MRS. CRANE: Oh, no! You don't suppose she went down there, do you?

Ms. COLLINS: Sally is too sensible to do anything so dangerous.

MRS. CRANE: But you don't know how much she wants to be a sourdough. She'd try anything. I'm going down there right away.

Ms. COLLINS: Why don't you call, instead? Mr. Smith can stop her in time.

MRS. CRANE: Good idea. (MRS. CRANE *flips through phone book, finds number, dials.*) I hope Sally's all right! *(Into phone)* Hello, Mr. Smith? . . . This is Mrs. Crane. Have you seen my daughter Sally down there? . . . What's that? . . . Oh, no! (SALLY *enters, smiling. She wears coat, carries envelope.*)

ALL *(Ad lib):* Sally! Are you O.K.? *(Etc.)*

MRS. CRANE *(Into phone):* Never mind, Mr. Smith. She just came in. *(Hangs up; angrily)* Sally Crane, where have you been?

SALLY: I just went down to the Trading Post.

SOURDOUGH CHARLIE: Don't tell me you tried to pat that grizzly!

SALLY: I not only tried, I did it! Oh, Ms. Collins! I'm so glad you're here. You can read my letter from Mr. Smith to prove I really patted a grizzly.

MS. COLLINS *(Reading):* "This is to certify that Sally Crane patted a real, full-grown grizzly at the Trading Post on this last of April, 19--. Signed, Preston R. Smith, Proprietor."

MRS. CRANE: Sally, you might have been killed.

SALLY: Oh, no! The grizzly was dead! There was nothing in the rules that said the grizzly had to be alive. I just patted that old stuffed one Mr. Smith has had for twenty years.

DAISY *(Laughing):* You really played a trick on us!

SALLY: And now you can't call me a *Chee-cha-ko* any more. I'm a real sourdough like the rest of you.

MS. COLLINS: What you don't know, Sally, is that you have been an honest-to-goodness sourdough for the past week.

SALLY *(Puzzled):* How? I don't understand.

MS. COLLINS: The real test of a sourdough is that he must live through an Alaskan winter from one spring ice break to another. When that ice began to melt last week, you and your whole family became official sourdoughs.

SALLY: But why didn't somebody tell me?

DAISY: It was a secret.

MS. COLLINS: The students voted that you are one of the most loyal Alaskans in our school and should, therefore, have the honor of making the closing speech about our flag.

SALLY: You mean I am going to be Miss Alaska?

ALL *(Ad lib):* Yes, you are! We all voted for you! *(Etc.)*

SALLY: Oh, I can hardly believe it! Thank you! Thank you! This is the happiest day of my life.

MRS. CRANE: That's wonderful, dear! And now I think it's time I got those cookies. *(She exits.)*

Ms. COLLINS: And I think it's high time for us to have a rehearsal. Sourdough Charlie, make your speech.

SOURDOUGH CHARLIE *(Stepping forward with a bow):* Ladies and gentlemen, as the final number of our spring program, we will have a tribute to the Alaskan state flag by Miss Alaska herself, otherwise known as Sourdough Sally!

SALLY *(Stepping up to painting of flag):* This beautiful flag which we all love and respect was designed by a thirteen-year-old Indian boy named Benny Benson. When Benny designed our flag, he was a seventh-grade pupil at the Mission School in Seward. His design was officially adopted by our legislature in 1927. Today our Alaskan flag takes its place with the flags of the other states in the union. So wherever this flag flies, Alaskans are reminded of their love of country and their pride in the last frontier.

Alaska's flag is filled with stars,
The Dipper points the way
To where the North Star holds its place,
A steady, shining ray.
The North Star is a friendly guide
To sailors lost at sea,
To trappers lost in fields of snow,
And even you and me.

Alaska's flag, a beacon light,
A flag we all hold dear,
Its eight gold stars on field of blue,
Salute the last frontier.
(All sing "God Bless America" as curtains close.)

THE END

The Paper Bag Mystery

Characters

BENNY
JOE
JUDY ⎫
CINDY ⎪
PAM ⎬ *Girl Scouts*
NELL ⎪
SUSAN ⎪
DIANE ⎭
MISS ENDERS, *Girl Scout leader*
MR. FOX (FOXY), *school janitor*
LT. RITA MURRAY ⎫ *police officers*
LT. JOHN STUART ⎭
MR. DIEHL

SETTING: *Office in a deserted school building. There are three desks and several chairs right. A safe with combination lock is against left wall.*

AT RISE: *Stage is empty. Banging and pounding are heard from offstage. After short pause, BENNY and JOE enter. JOE carries a large paper bag. BENNY has two pairs of coveralls over his arm, which conceal a paper bag, and carries dust mop and dustpan.*

51

JOE: Say, Benny, that janitor we locked in the basement sure is making a lot of noise. *(Puts bag on first desk)*

BENNY *(Putting mop and dustpan down)*: No one else can hear him. This old school is completely deserted.

JOE: Are you sure?

BENNY: Positive. They're tearing it down next month. *(Puts paper bag on another desk)*

JOE *(Persistently)*: Then why do they still have a janitor?

BENNY *(Impatiently)*: I don't know. Anyhow, with him locked up in the boiler room, we have the place to ourselves. We can stash the jewels in the safe and hide out here for the weekend until the commotion dies down.

JOE: Great! Now, where's the food? I'm starved.

BENNY *(Pointing)*: It's in that bag.

JOE: But I thought the jewels were in the bag.

BENNY *(Impatiently)*: They are, Joe. They're in the bag I was carrying. You carried the bag with the food in it.

JOE: Oh. *(Opens bag on desk near him and looks inside)* Bananas and ham sandwiches. *(Pulls out sandwich, begins to eat it)* Now let's have a look at the loot.

BENNY: O.K. *(Throws coveralls onto desk, opens second paper bag, and pulls out sparkling necklace)* How do you like that?

JOE: Wow! What a string of ice!

BENNY: Worth a fortune, this is. A single one of those stones will see us safely out of the country.

JUDY *(Calling from off)*: Mr. Fox, we're here! Hello!

BENNY: Someone's coming! Quick! Get out of sight!

JOE *(Putting necklace back into bag)*: Open the safe! Hurry! *(As BENNY kneels in front of safe, JOE puts paper bag containing jewels on chair.)*

BENNY *(Turning dial of combination lock)*: It's a good thing I know the combination!

JOE: Hurry up!

BENNY: There's something wrong! This safe door won't open.

JUDY *(Calling again, louder, from offstage):* Mr. Fox! Yoo-hoo, Mr. Fox!

BENNY: Hurry! Get into a pair of those coveralls, quick! *(As* JOE *struggles to put on coveralls)* I'll need more time.

JOE *(With coveralls half on):* We've got to get out of here!

BENNY *(Rising):* On the double. We can duck into a classroom. Grab that mop and dustpan, and let's go! *(He grabs second pair of coveralls and bag with lunch from top of desk. They dash off left,* JOE *still struggling with coveralls.* JUDY *enters through door, right, carrying paper bag.)*

JUDY: The door's open. (NELL, SUSAN, DIANE, CINDY, *and* PAM *enter, in Scout uniforms.* CINDY *and* PAM *carry large cardboard carton between them. Others carry paper bags, which they put on first desk.)*

NELL: Good old Foxy! He said he'd have everything ready for us.

SUSAN: I wonder where he is?

DIANE: He's around someplace, Sue.

CINDY *(As she and* PAM *put box on desk at front):* This box is heavy!

JUDY: I'll move these lunch bags out of the way, so you'll have more room.

NELL: I'll give you a hand, Judy. (JUDY *and* NELL *put lunch bags on second desk.)*

PAM *(Noticing paper bag on chair):* Here's somebody's lunch. I'll put it with the others. *(Places bag containing jewels with lunch bags on second desk)*

JUDY *(Looking into box):* No wonder this box is so

heavy. *(Taking out large pack of folded paper bags)* We have enough odds and ends in here to fill a thousand grab bags. We should be able to make a lot of money selling them at our Scout Fair!

CINDY: I can get more bags if we need them, Judy. Mr. Burns at the grocery store said we may have as many as we need. He even gave me some candy for the grab bags.

DIANE: I wish more people were like Mr. Burns. That grouchy Mr. Diehl down at the jewelry store won't even let me put a poster in his window.

SUSAN: He *is* a grouch! He's the one on the City Council who won't go along with leasing this building to the Girl Scouts. He said that the Girl Scouts would run down the property. *(Banging and pounding are heard from offstage.)*

PAM: What's that?

NELL: It seems to be coming from the basement.

SUSAN: Maybe we should check it out.

PAM: Not me! I wouldn't go there for the world.

JUDY: Oh, Pam, really! I think you've been watching too many late-night movies.

NELL: Besides, Mr. Fox is around here somewhere, and Miss Enders should be here any minute.

DIANE: The banging is probably just the heat coming up in these old pipes.

PAM: I wish Mr. Fox would show up.

JUDY: Mr. Fox or no Mr. Fox, we'd better get to work if we're going to fill these grab bags before lunch.

CINDY: Speaking of lunch . . . I'm hungry.

DIANE *(Pointing to second desk):* The lunches are all over there on that desk. *(As CINDY goes to lunch bags)* I'll open up these empty bags and put all of our stuff out on the desk, so we can fill the grab bags. (DIANE *and* PAM *take various items from box.*)

SUSAN *(Examining items):* Life Savers, ballpoint pens, nail polish, stickers . . .

DIANE: Beads, bracelets, pins . . . We seem to have more jewelry than anything else.

CINDY *(Holding banana in one hand, bag of jewels in another):* And here's some more jewelry—a whole bag full here with our lunch bags.

PAM: That's the one I picked off the chair. I thought it was somebody's lunch.

JUDY: Just put that jewelry with the rest. (CINDY *empties bag of real jewels onto desk.*) This looks much nicer than the rest of the costume jewelry.

SUSAN *(Holding up necklace):* It sure does! Isn't this gorgeous?

JUDY: It looks real.

DIANE: They're making great imitations these days.

NELL: How do we go about dividing all this up?

JUDY: Just be sure each bag has a little of everything. *(Girls begin to put various articles into bags.)*

SUSAN *(Taking twist ties from carton and sitting at third desk):* You girls fill the bags, and I'll put these ties on them. *(Girls fill bags and take them to* SUSAN's *desk during following dialogue.)*

NELL: I wonder who gave that necklace and all those pretty rings and bracelets?

CINDY: Probably Miss Enders. She said she was going to collect some stuff. She must have left it here earlier.

NELL: I wonder where she is.

PAM: Probably in the gym decorating the booths Mr. Fox put up yesterday.

JUDY: I guess that's why these doors were open. (MISS ENDERS *enters, wearing Scout uniform and carrying several bags and packages.*)

MISS ENDERS: Sorry I'm late, girls, but there was a terrible traffic jam on Main Street. *(Puts packages on desk)* I see Mr. Fox had everything ready for you.

NELL: We haven't seen Mr. Fox, Miss Enders.

MISS ENDERS: Then how did you get in?

PAM: The building was open.

MISS ENDERS: The office, too? *(Girls nod.)* Strange. Mr. Fox is usually so careful. I've never known him to leave the building open. *(Looking into grab bags)* Well! *(Holding up bracelet)* Who brought this lovely jewelry?

JUDY: It was here when we came.

CINDY: We thought you'd left it here for us.

MISS ENDERS *(Opening one of her bags):* I brought a few pieces of jewelry, but nothing as nice as those rings and pins. . . . I think I'll look around for Mr. Fox before I go up to the gym. He may not have unlocked it yet. (BENNY *and* JOE *enter left, wearing coveralls.* JOE *carries mop and dustpan.*)

BENNY: That won't be necessary, ma'am. Foxy won't be here today.

MISS ENDERS: And who are you?

BENNY: I'm Foxy's nephew, Benny, and this is my friend Joe. Foxy called us this morning and asked us to cover for him here. His back went out on him while he was working—he strained a muscle or something.

MISS ENDERS: I hope he didn't hurt himself putting up those booths.

BENNY: Uncle Foxy's not as young as he used to be.

MISS ENDERS: We'll have to be more thoughtful of him in the future. *(To* BENNY) Do you happen to know if the gym is unlocked?

BENNY: Yes, the gym doors are open.

MISS ENDERS: Good. *(To girls)* Now, if you girls are just

about finished with the grab bags, I could use some help decorating the gym.

CINDY: Do you think we should get some more bags from Mr. Burns?

MISS ENDERS: Yes, that's a good idea, Cindy. Grab bags always go fast.

JUDY: I'll go along to help Cindy, Miss Enders.

MISS ENDERS: Fine, Judy. (*To* BENNY) Benny, would you and Joe mind looking after things here? It would be a big help.

BENNY: Not at all, ma'am.

MISS ENDERS: Thanks very much. (*To girls*) O.K., girls—let's go to the gym. (*They start out.*)

CINDY (*As she and others exit*): I'll see you when I get back.

JUDY (*Exiting last*): Wait for me, Cindy!

BENNY (*As soon as girls have left*): Just our luck to have this place crawling with Girl Scouts! Now, quick, Joe— tell me where you left that bag with the jewels!

JOE (*Pointing to chair*): Right there on that chair.

BENNY (*Looking*): Well, it's not here now!

JOE (*Pointing to lunch bags on desk*): Maybe it's here with these bags. (*Opens one*) Nope . . . lunch! (*Examining others*) More lunch! These girls must be big eaters.

BENNY: Look at all those paper bags! The jewels could be in any one of them!

JOE: What are we going to do?

BENNY: We'll just have to open all the bags, look through them, and tie them again. We don't want those Girl Scouts suspecting us of anything. (*They begin untying and looking into bags.* JUDY *re-enters with* CINDY *and* PAM.)

JUDY: Hey! What are you doing with those bags?

BENNY *(Startled):* Nothing, miss. Er—the ties seemed to be a bit loose.

JUDY: We'll take care of them. Miss Enders wants both of you in the gym, right away.

JOE: But we can't go now . . . we have some—er—work to do here.

BENNY *(Taking his arm):* Come on, Joe. You heard what the young lady said. *(As* BENNY *and* JOE *exit, offstage pounding resumes, this time in Morse Code SOS pattern—three short beats, three long, then three short.)*

JUDY *(Puzzled):* Cindy—Pam—there's something funny going on here.

CINDY: Do you mean that banging?

PAM: It doesn't sound like radiators to me.

JUDY: Not only the banging, but the unlocked building . . . those men. I think they're up to something.

PAM: Why?

JUDY: Because Foxy couldn't have strained a muscle putting up those flimsy booths.

PAM: He's always bragging about how he can lift more than men half his age.

JUDY: And that's not all. He said Foxy called them from here. That's not possible; the phone has been disconnected for a week.

CINDY *(As pounding continues):* Listen. . . . Doesn't that sound familiar? *(Girls listen as pounding is heard again in SOS pattern.)* That's the Morse Code for SOS. And it sounds as if it's coming from the boiler room!

PAM: I'll go downstairs and find out what's going on. *(Exits left)*

JUDY: Cindy, I'm scared. We should get help.

CINDY: I'll go get Miss Enders. *(As she dashes off right,* JOE *and* BENNY *re-enter right, and* CINDY *runs into them.)*

BENNY: Hey! Where are you going in such a hurry?

JUDY *(Quickly):* She has to get some more paper bags.

CINDY *(Flustered):* Yes. We've run out of them.

JOE *(Sarcastically):* Oh, sure, that's just what you need—more paper bags.

BENNY *(To* JOE): Keep quiet, you dope.

JUDY *(With meaningful glance at* CINDY): Listen, Cindy, if Mr. Burns isn't there, be sure to talk to his brother.

CINDY *(Puzzled):* His brother?

JUDY: Yes, his brother Timothy. He'll send us exactly what we need.

CINDY *(Suddenly catching on):* Oh, sure! Timothy is Mr. Burns's right-hand man. O.K., Judy. Don't worry. I'll get just what we need.

JUDY: And hurry! We want to finish up here before lunch! (CINDY *runs out.*)

BENNY: What's in all these paper bags, anyway, miss?

JUDY: Odds and ends the Girl Scouts have collected. Our troop is in charge of the grab bags at the Scout Fair this year.

BENNY *(Picking up a bag):* How much are you charging for them?

JUDY: Twenty-five cents.

BENNY *(Surprised):* Twenty-five cents!

JUDY: Is that too much?

BENNY *(Smiling craftily):* No, not at all. In fact, I've just been thinking of offering to buy the whole lot.

JUDY: But that would spoil the fun!

BENNY: Suppose I were to offer you thirty cents a bag, for the whole lot? That way you'd make more money for your troop.

JUDY *(Uneasily):* I don't know. I don't think that would be right. They're counting on this for the Scout Fair.

BENNY: Suppose I make it forty cents a bag, or even

fifty cents? I like to support the Scouts.

JUDY: I'd have to ask Miss Enders. She wouldn't want us to charge that much.

BENNY: Suppose I insist?

JUDY *(Frightened):* What do you mean?

JOE *(Impatiently):* Oh, for Pete's sake, Benny, why don't you cut out all the double talk and just take the bags? We have to get out of here. (PAM *and* FOXY *enter, unnoticed.* FOXY *carries a long-handled mop.)* There's nobody here to stop us!

FOXY: I'm not so sure about that.

JUDY *(Turning, seeing* FOXY *and* PAM): Foxy! Pam!

JOE: The old guy's got himself untied. *(Snatching up as many bags as he can carry)* Out of my way, old man, I'm coming through! (FOXY *flails about with mop.)*

BENNY *(Also snatching up bags):* We were too easy on you the first time. *(Gives* FOXY *a push that sends him sprawling.* BENNY *and* JOE *dash out right.)*

JUDY: Oh, Foxy! Are you hurt? *(Runs over to him)*

FOXY *(Picking himself up):* Only my pride! That's the second time today those thieves have gotten the best of me!

JUDY: Thieves?

FOXY: Yes, Judy. They robbed Diehl's Jewelry Store this morning.

PAM *(Excitedly):* Judy, those rings and necklaces *were* the real thing, after all!

JUDY *(Alarmed):* And now the thieves have gotten away! *(There is scuffle in doorway, and* LT. STUART *and* LT. MURRAY *enter with* BENNY *and* JOE, *who still clutch paper bags.)*

MURRAY: Put those bags on the desk, you two. (BENNY *and* JOE *do so.)*

STUART: Now, hands up, both of you!

CINDY *(Rushing in, breathlessly):* Oh, thank goodness the police arrived in time! Chief Burns called the cruiser right away. (MISS ENDERS *enters with* NELL, DIANE, *and* SUSAN.)

MISS ENDERS: What in the world is going on here? *(Sees* FOXY) Mr. Fox! I thought you were ill!

FOXY: No such thing, Miss Enders—just tied up down in the boiler room till the girls caught on to my SOS signal and came to the rescue.

NELL: So that's what all the banging was about!

FOXY: I was banging on the pipes. When I remembered you girls were studying signaling in your scouting manual, I decided to try Morse Code.

MISS ENDERS: Please tell me what has happened! Why are the police here?

MURRAY *(Pointing to* JOE *and* BENNY): These two characters robbed Diehl's Jewelry Store this morning.

MISS ENDERS *(Shocked):* Good heavens!

STUART: They were hiding out here, but one of your students notified Chief Burns, and he called the squad car.

CINDY: It was Judy's idea, Miss Enders. She told me to go to Mr. Burns's brother, and it finally dawned on me that Timothy Burns is the Chief of Police! (MR. DIEHL *enters, wildly excited.)*

MR. DIEHL: Chief Burns just called me! Where are the thieves? Let me get my hands on them!

STUART: Everything is under control, Mr. Diehl.

MURRAY: We just want you to identify these men so we can take them down to headquarters. *(Indicates* BENNY *and* JOE)

MR. DIEHL: They're the ones, all right. I'd know them anywhere. But where are the jewels?

JUDY: Right here, Mr. Diehl. *(Indicating bags)*

PAM: You'll have to look through all the bags to find them, though.

DIANE: We didn't know the necklace and the pins and other jewels were real, so we put a few in each bag.

NELL: We thought it was all costume jewelry.

MR. DIEHL: Costume jewelry! Those are the finest pieces in my shop!

MURRAY (*To* JOE *and* BENNY): All right, you two—let's go!

MR. DIEHL: I'll be down to sign charges against them as soon as I find the jewels. Thank you for your quick action, Officers.

MURRAY: Don't thank us, Mr. Diehl. Thank the Girl Scouts!

STUART: That's right. If it hadn't been for them, these two would have escaped. (MURRAY *and* STUART *exit with* BENNY *and* JOE.)

MR. DIEHL: What did you Girl Scouts have to do with this?

FOXY *(Quickly):* They had plenty to do with it, Mr. Diehl. If they hadn't learned Morse Code in their scout troop, they never would have recognized my SOS.

CINDY: And it was Judy who sent me to Chief Burns for help.

MISS ENDERS *(Proudly):* These Girl Scouts are just living up to the Girl Scout Law—and a Girl Scout's duty is to help others.

MR. DIEHL: Miss Enders, you and I have been on opposite sides of the fence about leasing this building to the Scouts, but what I've seen here today has changed my mind. I'm going to go back and recommend to the City Council that they go ahead with it. I'll even donate the reward money for the return of the jewels to your rent fund.

GIRLS *(Ad lib):* That's great! Wonderful! Thank you! *(Etc.)*

MISS ENDERS: Thank you, Mr. Diehl. I promise you'll never regret it.

MR. DIEHL *(Holding out his hand):* Let's shake on that, Miss Enders.

SUSAN *(As* MISS ENDERS *extends her hand):* Give him the Girl Scout handshake, Miss Enders. (MISS EN-DERS *gives* MR. DIEHL *Girl Scout handshake, which is repeated by others, as curtains close.)*

THE END

The Trial of Mother Goose

Characters

Old King Cole
Queen
Cook
Mary, *the maid*
Peter, *the pipe-maker*
Felix ⎫
Freddy ⎬ *fiddlers*
Fritz ⎭
Mother Goose
Mistress Mary
Little Boy Blue
Miss Muffet
Jenny
Tom, the Piper's Son
The Old Woman in the Shoe
Two Soldiers
Herald
Twelve Children
Prince George

Setting: *The kitchen of King Cole's palace. A long table covered with a cloth stands center, with benches on either side, and a high-backed chair at one end.*

AT RISE: COOK *is stirring stew in iron pot at fireplace right.* MARY, *at worktable left, is polishing a silver bowl.* PETER *sits on fireplace stool, carving a new pipe.*

MARY *(Holding up bowl):* There! It's as bright as I can make it.

COOK: Why are you working so hard, Mary? King Cole hasn't called for his bowl in weeks.

MARY: I want to have it ready, just in case.

PETER: That's why I'm making this new pipe. He must be tired of his old ones. He never sends for them anymore! (FELIX, FREDDY *and* FRITZ *enter left, carrying their fiddles.*)

FELIX: Um-m-m! Something smells good. *(Approaching* COOK) May I have a taste? *(Reaches for pot)*

COOK *(Slapping his hand):* Out of my way, Felix. This is no place for three lazy fiddlers.

FRITZ: But we're not lazy at all. It's not our fault the King hasn't called for us in a month of Sundays.

FREDDY: We came to help. Isn't there something we can do?

FELIX: Freddy and I could fill the wood box, and Fritz could help with the dishes.

FRITZ: Or set the table, or shell the peas!

FELIX: I'd even peel potatoes, anything for something to do.

PETER: Why don't you go practice your scales or write a new tune?

FREDDY: What's the use? King Cole wouldn't even let us play it.

COOK *(Shaking her head):* The King is not himself these days. Nothing pleases him these days.

ALL *(Reciting sadly and slowly):*
> Old King Cole is a grumpy old soul,

And a grumpy old soul is he.
He *won't* have his pipe,
And he *won't* have his bowl,
And he *won't* have his fiddlers three!
(QUEEN *enters right during last lines, wiping her eyes with a flowing handkerchief.*)

QUEEN *(Tearfully):* And the King won't even talk to me!

ALL *(Bowing and curtsying):* Your Majesty!

FREDDY: We were not making fun of His Majesty.

FRITZ: But the King really is grumpy.

COOK: There's no pleasing him.

MARY: The truth is, we're worried about him.

QUEEN: So am I! Cole was always such a dear, merry soul. And now he hardly ever laughs or smiles. *(Weeps)*

COOK *(Helping her to chair at head of table):* There, there, Your Majesty! Let me make you a cup of tea. *(Busies herself filling a cup at fireplace)*

FRITZ: Let us play a tune for you. Perhaps it would cheer you up.

QUEEN: No thank you, Fritz. I couldn't bear it.

PETER: The King has everything to make him happy.

MARY: Not an enemy in the world!

QUEEN: But that's just the trouble. He claims he *does* have an enemy! An enemy who must be hunted down and brought to him in chains before he ever smiles again.

ALL: Who is it?

QUEEN: I have no idea!

MARY: Everybody in the Kingdom loves Old King Cole.

QUEEN: If only he would believe that! *(Knocking on door left is heard.)*

MOTHER GOOSE *(Calling from off left):* Let me in! Help! Let me in!

COOK: Quick! Open the door! *(*PETER *runs left to open door, and* MOTHER GOOSE *rushes in, looking over her shoulder in fear.)*

MOTHER GOOSE *(Upset):* Oh, please, hide me! Hide me! They're after me! They're right on my heels!

QUEEN: Do not be afraid. You are among friends. *(Rising and helping* MOTHER GOOSE *to bench)* Sit down and calm yourself. Now—who are you, and who is hunting for you?

MOTHER GOOSE: The King's soldiers are after me!

FELIX: What have you done?

MOTHER GOOSE: I have done nothing to harm a soul. I am only a poor, old woman, helpless and alone.

QUEEN: What is your name?

MOTHER GOOSE: My name is Mother Goose, and all my life I have written verses for children. Oh, please, Your Majesty, take pity on me and protect me from the soldiers. *(Loud pounding is heard on door left.)*

1ST SOLDIER *(Shouting from off left):* Open in the King's name!

MOTHER GOOSE: The soldiers! Hide me!

QUEEN: Quick! Under the table! (MOTHER GOOSE *ducks under table, as* QUEEN *and* MARY *pull the tablecloth over the edge to hide her.* TWO SOLDIERS *burst in left.)*

1ST SOLDIER: Where is she?

2ND SOLDIER: We saw her come in here!

1ST SOLDIER: Hand her over!

2ND SOLDIER: By order of the King!

QUEEN: Gentlemen, you forget yourselves. You are in the presence of your Queen. *(They drop to knees.)*

1ST SOLDIER: Pardon, Your Gracious Majesty, pardon.

QUEEN: Now, what is the meaning of this? *(They rise.)*

2ND SOLDIER: We were on the trail of an enemy of the King, Your Majesty.

1ST SOLDIER: He ordered us to bring her in, dead or alive.

QUEEN: You must be mistaken. Such a poor, harmless old woman!

2ND SOLDIER: Your Majesty *has* seen her.

1ST SOLDIER: Then she *did* come in here.

FELIX: Shall we throw them out, Your Majesty? There are six of us against two of them. (COOK *raises a saucepan aloft,* MARY *raises her bowl,* PETER *brandishes his wooden pipe, and fiddlers lift their violins in a threatening manner.*)

PETER: Just say the word, Your Majesty! (KING COLE *rushes in right, followed by* HERALD, *who carries scroll and pen.*)

KING COLE: What is the meaning of this? What goes on here?

1ST SOLDIER: We trailed the old woman through the palace grounds, sire.

2ND SOLDIER: She must be hiding in this very room.

KING COLE: Then find her! What are you waiting for? (HERALD *and* SOLDIERS *search.*)

QUEEN: Sire, I will not stand by and see a harmless old woman hunted down by these ruffians. *(The table shakes and moves.)*

HERALD *(Pointing):* Look! Look, Your Majesty! The table! *(All watch table. Again it shakes and moves noticeably.)*

KING COLE: Aha! *(He pulls off tablecloth and bends over.* MOTHER GOOSE *is kneeling under table.)* So there you are!

QUEEN: Please, sire, let her go!

MOTHER GOOSE *(Coming out):* It's no use, ma'am!

KING COLE: Guard the prisoner, men. *(Seats himself in*

chair; HERALD *stands beside him.* SOLDIERS *hold* MOTHER GOOSE *between them.)* Herald, read the charges against this woman.

HERALD *(Reading from scroll):* The prisoner is charged with writing silly, stupid, and insulting verses about His Majesty, King Cole, members of the Royal Family, and many important citizens.

KING COLE: You have heard the charges, Mother Goose. How do you plead? Guilty or innocent?

MOTHER GOOSE: I admit writing many verses, Your Majesty, but I deny that they are silly, stupid, or insulting.

KING COLE: Make a note, Herald. *(As* HERALD *writes)* She admits writing the verses. We will now take up that ridiculous rhyme she wrote about me.

QUEEN: Everyone knows that, sire.
"Old King Cole was a merry old soul,
And a merry old soul was he . . .

PETER: "He called for his pipe . . .

MARY: "He called for his bowl . . .

FIDDLERS: "And he called for his fiddlers three!"

QUEEN: Now what is so silly or insulting about that?

KING COLE: It makes me look foolish. Wasting my time eating, drinking, and listening to music. I want the world to know about my great deeds—the damsels in distress I've rescued, the fine laws I've made, the battles I've won. *(Petulantly)* Besides, I am not old. I'm only thirty-nine!

MOTHER GOOSE: But, Your Majesty . . .

KING COLE: Quiet! The Herald will now read what she wrote about our son, Prince George.

HERALD *(Reading):*
"Georgie Porgie, pudding and pie,

Kissed the girls and made them cry!" *(All laugh.)*

KING COLE: Silence! I will not allow you to laugh at our son.

QUEEN: But you know Georgie *is* always kissing the girls.

KING COLE: I also know they don't cry. At least, not many of them. Herald, it's time for the witnesses. You may show them in. (HERALD *moves right, announces names in loud voice. As each name is called, the witness enters right and faces audience.)*

HERALD: Mistress Mary! Little Boy Blue! Little Miss Muffet! Jenny! Tom, the Piper's Son! The Old Woman in the Shoe!

KING COLE: Mistress Mary, what is your complaint against Mother Goose?

MISTRESS MARY (*Pointing at* MOTHER GOOSE): Everybody calls me "Contrary Mary" because of that silly rhyme she wrote:
"Mistress Mary, quite contrary,
How does your garden grow?"

KING COLE: Little Boy Blue, what is your complaint?

LITTLE BOY BLUE (*Pointing):* I can't get a job. No one will hire me to mind the sheep, because *she* said I was under a haystack fast asleep.

KING COLE: Little Miss Muffet will state her case.

MISS MUFFET (*Pointing):* Folks think I'm a fraidy-cat because *she* said I ran away from a spider.

KING COLE: Jenny, what is your charge against this woman?

JENNY (*Pointing):* I can earn only a penny a day, because she said I can't work any faster.

KING COLE: Tom, the Piper's Son, is our next witness.

TOM (*Pointing):* I was beaten for stealing one little old pig.

KING COLE: Our final witness is the Old Woman Who Lived in a Shoe.

OLD WOMAN *(Pointing):* People think I'm cruel to my children. She wrote that I gave them some broth, without any bread, and whipped them all soundly and sent them to bed.

KING COLE: You have heard the complaints against you, Mother Goose. What do you have to say for yourself?

MOTHER GOOSE: Nothing, Your Majesty. I only wrote the truth.

KING COLE: In that case, the trial is ended. You stand guilty as accused.

QUEEN, MARY, PETER *and* FIDDLERS: No, no, Your Majesty! Have mercy!

KING COLE: I repeat! The court finds you guilty, but because I am a just and kindly man, I will give you one more chance.

QUEEN: Thank you, thank you, sire.

KING COLE: I have asked each one of our witnesses, before coming into court, to prepare his own version of his case. If you will sign these new rhymes I have written down here *(Takes out papers)* and agree to have them printed in every Mother Goose book from now on, we will set you free. Do you agree?

MOTHER GOOSE: Before I decide, I must hear the rhymes.

KING COLE: Very well. We will start with Mistress Mary.

MISTRESS MARY:
Mistress Mary, light and airy,
How does your garden grow?
With cockle shells and silver bells,
And pretty maids all in a row.

LITTLE BOY BLUE:
Little Boy Blue is blowing his horn

To keep the animals out of the corn.
He is the one to look after your sheep,
Always alert, and never asleep!

MISS MUFFET:

Little Miss Muffet, she sat on a tuffet,
Eating of curds and whey.
There came a great spider, who sat down beside her,
But bravely, Miss Muffet did stay!

JENNY:

See-saw, Margery Daw,
Jenny shall have a new master;
She must earn more than a penny a day,
Because she works faster and faster!

OLD WOMAN:

There was a good woman who lived in a shoe;
For children she always knew just what to do.
She fed them their supper and put them to bed,
Giving each little darling a pat on the head!

KING COLE: In the absence of Prince George, I have
written the following: *(Reading from papers)*
The young Prince George had a charming way
Of kissing the girls to make them stay!
And as for myself, I have composed what I think you
will agree is a masterpiece:
Great King Cole was a mighty fine soul,
And a mighty fine soul was he!
He called for his sword,
And he called for his gun,
And he marched off to victory!
(Gives papers to HERALD)

HERALD *(Bringing papers to* MOTHER GOOSE): Just sign
here, my good woman.

MOTHER GOOSE: Never! Never! Never! I would rather be put in the dungeon forever than sign such a pack of lies and falsehoods.

KING COLE *(Angrily):* Then you will go to the dungeon! You have had your chance. *(To* SOLDIERS) To the dungeon with her!

QUEEN *and* SERVANTS: No! No! No! No!

CHILDREN *(Chanting from off left):* No! No! No! No! *(If desired,* CHILDREN *may be seated in audience and come up on stage at* KING COLE's *command.)*

KING COLE: What is this shouting?

QUEEN *(Moving left):* Out there, Your Majesty.

KING COLE *(Going left and peering off):* Where? I can't see anyone. *(Calls off loudly)* Come here where I can see you. (PRINCE GEORGE, *disguised as a peasant, enters left, followed by* TWELVE CHILDREN. KING COLE *sits in chair.*) Who are you who dare defy me? What do you want?

2ND CHILD: We demand justice for Mother Goose.

3RD CHILD: We want to be heard.

PRINCE GEORGE: Mother Goose belongs to the children of the world, and we are here to defend her.

1ST CHILD: We want no change in Mother Goose!

MISTRESS MARY: But our new rhymes are ever so much better than the old ones.

PRINCE GEORGE: That's because you're too contrary to see the difference.

MISTRESS MARY *(Stamping her foot):* I am not contrary!

4TH CHILD: Yes, you are! That's why we love you.

5TH CHILD: That's why you're famous.

MISTRESS MARY *(In amazement):* Me? Famous?

PRINCE GEORGE: Of course. Mother Goose has made every one of you famous all over the world.

6TH CHILD:

> From Zanzibar to Londonderry,
> The children love Contrary Mary!

7TH CHILD:

> In China, India, and Peru,
> The children sing about Boy Blue!

LITTLE BOY BLUE: And don't they mind that I fell asleep?

8TH CHILD: They wouldn't like you half so much if you had stayed awake.

MISS MUFFET: And what about me? Do they make fun of me because I ran away from a spider?

9TH CHILD: No, lots of people are afraid of spiders.

TOM: I'll bet they don't like me because I stole that pig.

CHILDREN *(Together):* Oh, yes, they do!

PRINCE GEORGE:

> Many children make mistakes,
> Some little, and some big.
> And we are sure you never stole
> Another little pig!

TOM: You're so right! I learned my lesson.

10TH CHILD:

> And as for Jenny standing here,
> Although we went right past her,

11TH CHILD:

> We like her just the way she is!
> We wouldn't want her faster!

OLD WOMAN: How about me? Do children know I really love them?

12TH CHILD:

> Our mothers love us very much,
> On that we're always banking.
> But also every now and then,
> I guess we do need spanking.

OLD WOMAN: If this is what the children of the world

think of us, Your Majesty, I move that all charges against Mother Goose be dismissed.

WITNESSES *(Ad lib):* Agreed! Yes! Let her go! *(Etc.)*

KING COLE: But what about me? And what about my son, Prince George?

PRINCE GEORGE: For goodness' sake, Father, don't you know me?

KING COLE: Never saw you before. Who are you?

PRINCE GEORGE *(Taking off hat and putting on crown):* I'm Georgie—Georgie Porgie, pudding and pie!

KING COLE *and* QUEEN: The Prince!

KING COLE: What are you doing in those clothes?

PRINCE GEORGE: I believe that a prince should go out and mingle with the people and get to know them. So I have been traveling around the land, talking to all the boys and girls.

KING COLE: And do you mean to say you don't mind that insulting rhyme?

PRINCE GEORGE: Georgie Porgie, pudding and pie? I like it! And I like the rhyme Mother Goose wrote about me.

KING COLE: Even the part about making the girls cry when you kiss them?

PRINCE GEORGE *(Laughing):* I don't think you know very much about girls, Father. *(Softly)* They only *pretend* to cry. Inside they're really full of giggles.

KING COLE: It's all very well for the rest of you to drop your charges against Mother Goose. But I am the King, and I demand to be treated with respect.

PRINCE GEORGE: But, Father, they love you best of all.

1ST CHILD: We read about lots of kings who have won great battles, but half the time, we can't even remember their names.

PRINCE GEORGE: In my travels, I've seen your statue in

gardens and parks.

2ND CHILD: It's hard to find a jolly king like you.

KING COLE *(Chuckling):* I'm beginning to feel a bit merry in spite of myself.

ALL: Three cheers for Old King Cole! *(All cheer.)*

KING COLE *(Rising):* Mother Goose, I apologize, and grant you a full pardon. *(More cheers)* Herald, I wish to make a proclamation. (HERALD *takes notes as* KING COLE *proclaims)*

> Hear ye! Hear ye! From this day,
> Mother Goose shall hold full sway.
> Honor her when she appears,
> Greet her with resounding cheers!
> Ring the bells from spire and steeple,
> Teach her verses to the people.
> Never once forget the name
> Of Mother Goose, who brought us fame!

MOTHER GOOSE *(Rising and curtsying to him):* Thank you, King Cole!

PRINCE GEORGE: Thank you, Father. When I grow up to be a king, I'm going to be just like you.

> I'll try to be a merry old soul,
> A merry old soul I'll be!
> I'll call for my pipe *(Beckons)*
> And I'll call for my bowl *(Beckons)*
> And I'll call for my fiddlers three!
> *(Beckons)*

KING COLE: That's fine, son. But right now, I'll give my own orders. *(Claps his hands once)* Peter, my pipe! (PETER *brings him the pipe. He pretends to puff and returns it to* PETER. *Claps his hands twice)* Mary, my bowl! *(As she hands it to him)* Mother Goose, here's to your health. *(Drains bowl and returns it to* MARY. *Claps hands three times)* And now, for my fiddlers three! *(As they step forward and bow)* I order you to play the merriest tune that you know, as we choose our partners for the Mother Goose Hop. *(With a bow to* MOTHER GOOSE*)* Madam, will you do me the honor? *(*PRINCE GEORGE *bows to* QUEEN, *as all choose partners and dance as violin music is played by fiddlers, or pantomimed to offstage recording. Curtain)*

THE END

The Return of Bobby Shafto

Characters

BOBBY SHAFTO
LORD MAYOR OF FLORABELLA
LADY MAGNOLIA
LADY MARIGOLD ⎱ *his daughters*
LADY MORNING GLORY ⎰
MAID MARJORIE
GARDENER, *Marjorie's father*
TWO SAILORS

SETTING: *A wharf in the port of Florabella. Several large packing cases are piled up right, and a small platform representing a pier is at left.*
AT RISE: TWO SAILORS, *carrying a large sea chest, enter left, followed by* BOBBY SHAFTO, *who is wearing a velvet cape and cap and long white stockings with silver buckles at the knee. As they reach center, the* SAILORS *put down chest.* SHAFTO *draws a deep breath and stretches his arms above his head.*
SHAFTO: It's good to be home in Florabella again.
1ST SAILOR: But it's been a good voyage, too, Master Shafto, and you have a great treasure to show for it.

SHAFTO: That's right. I, Robert Shafto, will be the richest man in Florabella, and the happiest, as soon as I claim my promised bride.

1ST SAILOR: But why did you have us row you ashore here, so early in the morning?

2ND SAILOR: The Lord Mayor of Florabella has planned a royal welcome for you in the main harbor, and a great ball is arranged in your honor.

SHAFTO: I must attend to a few matters before my return is made public, lad. *(Offstage singing of "Bobby Shafto," to the traditional tune, is heard.)* Quick! Someone is coming! Drag that chest behind those packing cases, men, and keep out of sight. *(*SHAFTO *and* SAILORS *hide chest and duck down behind boxes, as* LADY MAGNOLIA, *dressed in white and twirling a white parasol, enters and strolls up and down singing.)*

LADY MAGNOLIA:
Bobby Shafto's gone to sea,
Silver buckles on his knee.
He'll come back and marry me!
Handsome Bobby Shafto!

I can hardly wait for Bobby's return. His ship has been sighted, and in just a few hours, he'll be here. *(Offstage singing of "Bobby Shafto" is heard.)* Who is singing? Who *dares* sing my song? (LADY MARIGOLD *enters left, dressed in yellow with yellow parasol.)*

LADY MARIGOLD *(Singing):*
He'll come back and marry me!
Handsome Bobby Shafto! *(Sees* MAGNOLIA)

Good morning, sister Magnolia. I see you're up early. What a bright, breezy, beautiful day it is!

MAGNOLIA *(Grimly):* And it will be a dull, dark, dangerous day for you, sister Marigold, if you keep singing that song. Everybody knows Bobby Shafto belongs to *me!*

MARIGOLD: Is that so?

MAGNOLIA: Yes, that's so. *(They stare at each other suddenly, as song is heard offstage.)*

MARIGOLD *and* MAGNOLIA: Who's that? (LADY MORNING GLORY, *dressed in purple and carrying a purple parasol, enters left, singing last lines of "Bobby Shafto.")* Morning Glory!

LADY MORNING GLORY: Well, well, well! I never knew my dear sisters were such early risers! Are you planning to meet someone?

MARIGOLD: That song! That song you were singing just now!

MAGNOLIA: What right have you to sing of Bobby Shafto?

MORNING GLORY: Every right in the world! As the song says, "He'll come back and marry *me,* handsome Bobby Shafto!"

MAGNOLIA: He will not!

MARIGOLD: Indeed he won't!

MORNING GLORY: And why not, pray tell?

MARIGOLD *and* MAGNOLIA: Because he's going to marry *me!* *(All three glare at each other.)*

MORNING GLORY *(Folding her parasol):* Then two of us are making a mistake.

MAGNOLIA: Not me!

MARIGOLD: Not me!

MORNING GLORY: And what makes you so sure Bobby Shafto will marry *you,* sister Marigold?

MARIGOLD *(Folding parasol and producing a note from a little bag hanging from her wrist):*
This is the note he wrote to me
On the very day that he went to sea!

(Reading) "I promise you, dear Marigold,
More treasure than your arms can hold!"

MAGNOLIA *(Also folding parasol and producing note):*
And this is the note he wrote to *me*
On the very day that he went to sea!
(Reading) "Magnolia fair, I've gone to win
A fortune for you when my ship comes in!"

MORNING GLORY *(Also producing note):*
He also wrote such a note to me
On the very day that he went to sea.
(Reading) "Dear Morning Glory, bright and fair,
Some day my fortune you will share!"

MAGNOLIA: I don't care what he wrote to you, Morning
Glory! Or to you either, Marigold! I intend to marry
Bobby Shafto the minute he sets foot on this shore.

MARIGOLD: Not if I see him first, sister mine!

MORNING GLORY: You'll see! Bobby Shafto belongs to
me! *(The opening lines of "Bobby Shafto" are sung
offstage.)*

MAGNOLIA: Listen! Someone else is singing our song!
*(MAID MARJORIE enters, wearing a peasant costume,
and pushing cart piled high with fruits and vegetables)*

MARIGOLD: Stop that singing, Maid Marjorie.

MAID MARJORIE: What's the matter? What have I done?

MORNING GLORY: That song! We forbid you to sing it!

MAID MARJORIE: But I am so happy, I can't help singing.
Today will be my wedding day.

LADIES: Your *what?*

MAID MARJORIE: My wedding day! *(Singing)*
Bobby Shafto sailed away,
Promised he'd come home to stay!
This will be our wedding day!
Darling Bobby Shafto!

MAGNOLIA *(Laughing):* You silly girl! What makes you

think the rich and handsome Bobby Shafto would marry a beggar maid like you?

MAID MARJORIE: But I am not a beggar maid, Lady Magnolia. I make my own living, selling these fruits and vegetables from my father's garden.

MARIGOLD: It's *our* father's garden!

MAGNOLIA: Every acre of farmland in Florabella belongs to us—to the Lord Mayor and his family.

MAID MARJORIE: Alas, milady, this is true. But at one time, half of it belonged to our family. It is our dream to buy it back some day.

MAGNOLIA: Your dream is not likely to come true, Maid Marjorie.

MORNING GLORY: So you are really nothing but a beggar maid after all!

MAID MARJORIE (*With a toss of her head*): Beggar maid or no beggar maid, he promised to marry me.

MORNING GLORY: And what about his promise to me?

MAGNOLIA: And to me?

MARIGOLD: And to me?

MAID MARJORIE: I don't believe it!

MAGNOLIA: You'll believe it soon enough when the glad news is announced at the grand ball my father is planning for this evening.

MAID MARJORIE (*Tearfully*): He couldn't have promised anyone else but me!

MAGNOLIA: But he did! (*Shows letter*) And I have his letter to prove it.

MARIGOLD (*Showing letter*): And so have I!

MORNING GLORY (*Also showing letter*): And so have I!

MAID MARJORIE: And I was just on my way to the main harbor to meet him. His crew is already starting to come ashore.

MAGNOLIA: What? The ship is here?

MORNING GLORY: We must be there to greet him! *(Sisters rush off left.)*

MAID MARJORIE *(Sobbing):* Oh, Bobby! Bobby! How could you do such a dreadful thing! *(She pushes cart left and sinks down on the platform, leaning her cheek against the post, and sings sorrowfully)*

> Ever since you left my side,
> Sailing on the morning tide,
> I've waited here to be your bride,
> Darling Bobby Shafto!

(GARDENER enters right, walks in front of packing boxes.)

GARDENER: Marjorie! What are you doing here? Haven't you heard the news? Bobby Shafto's ship is sailing into the harbor.

MAID MARJORIE: I know, Father!

GARDENER: Then why aren't you there to greet him? What will he think of you?

MAID MARJORIE: I don't care what he thinks of me, Father. Not any more.

GARDENER: But you are to be his bride.

MAID MARJORIE: All the Lord Mayor's daughters are claiming the same thing.

GARDENER: What are you saying? Bobby Shafto is an honest lad. He would never make such a promise to all of you.

MAID MARJORIE: That's what I thought, Father. They showed me his letters.

GARDENER: Did you read them?

MAID MARJORIE: No, but . . .

GARDENER: Then do as I tell you. Dry your eyes and put on your brightest smile. You and I are going to be on hand when he returns. *(They exit left. SHAFTO and SAILORS enter from behind the boxes.)*

1ST SAILOR: Well, Master Shafto, you really do have yourself in a "picklement"!

2ND SAILOR: Four young ladies, all thinking you'll marry them!

SHAFTO: Easy, mates, easy! I can straighten everything out in a few minutes.

SAILORS: How?

SHAFTO: By keeping my promises, of course.

1ST SAILOR: How are you going to do that?

SHAFTO: Bring my sea chest to me, and I'll show you. Hurry! (SAILORS *exit.* SHAFTO *sits on floor, removes shoes and stockings, but holds silver buckles in his hand. He then rises and removes his cap and cloak.* SAILORS *bring sea chest onstage.*) Open the chest quickly! (*He stuffs his discarded clothing inside chest and takes out a ragged cloak and bandanna and an eye patch with string attached.*) Help me put these on, mates. (*They put on his eye patch and bandanna as* LORD MAYOR *enters left, followed by* LADY MAGNOLIA, LADY MARIGOLD, *and* LADY MORNING GLORY.)

LORD MAYOR: Where is he? Where is that scoundrel Shafto? How dare he insult the Lord Mayor by sneaking ashore without hearing my speech of welcome?

MAGNOLIA: Find him, Father!

MORNING GLORY: He's probably run away with that wretched beggar maid.

LORD MAYOR: What beggar maid?

MORNING GLORY: Maid Marjorie, the gardener's daughter. She thinks he is going to marry her.

MAGNOLIA: When he's already promised to marry me!

MARIGOLD: And me!

MORNING GLORY: And me!

LORD MAYOR: Wait till I get my hands on the wretch!

SHAFTO (*Advancing with a bow*): Perhaps I can help you, sir.

LORD MAYOR: If you know anything at all about this fellow Shafto, I will reward you handsomely.

SHAFTO: I know all about him, Your Lordship. It so happens that *I* am Bobby Shafto!

ALL: What!

SHAFTO: Bobby Shafto, at your service, sir.

MAGNOLIA: You're not Bobby Shafto!

MARIGOLD: Bobby Shafto's tall and fair!

MORNING GLORY: With bright blue eyes and golden hair!

LORD MAYOR: And it has come to my ears that Bobby Shafto made a fortune on this last voyage. You look more like a beggar lad than a merchant prince.

SHAFTO: Nevertheless, sir, my name is Robert Shafto, as my mates can testify. Speak up, lads.

1ST SAILOR: Aye, aye, sir.

2ND SAILOR: He's really Bobby Shafto, Your Honor.

SHAFTO: And I stand ready to keep my promises. (*Bowing to* MAGNOLIA) Lady Magnolia, my compliments!

MAGNOLIA (*Turning away*): Don't speak to me!

SHAFTO (*Bowing to* MARIGOLD): Lady Marigold . . .

MARIGOLD (*Turning away*): How dare you speak my name!

SHAFTO (*Bowing to* MORNING GLORY): Lady Morning Glory, surely you remember me.

MORNING GLORY: I never saw you before . . . nor do I wish to see you ever again! (MAID MARJORIE *enters left with* GARDENER. *She sees* SHAFTO, *runs to him.*)

MAID MARJORIE: Bobby! Bobby Shafto! Oh, I was so afraid something had happened to you.

SHAFTO: I promised I would come home again, Marjorie, and here I am.

LORD MAYOR: This fellow is an impostor! You are mistaken, Maid Marjorie.

MAID MARJORIE: Oh, no, sir! I could never be mistaken about Bobby Shafto. I'd know him anywhere.

GARDENER: And so would I. Welcome home, lad.

SHAFTO *(As they shake hands):* Thank you, sir. I knew my true friends would see through my disguise. *(Removes tattered cloak, revealing original costume)* Open the chest, lads. *(He removes eye patch and bandanna, tosses them into chest and puts on his velvet cap)* Now, ladies, do I look more like the Bobby Shafto you were expecting?

LADIES *(Ad lib):* Bobby! Bobby! It's really you! *(Etc.)*

SHAFTO *(Pointing to chest):* And here is the gold I promised, the fortune I made while I was away at sea.

ALL *(Crowding to look into chest; ad lib):* Gold! Bags of it! He's rich! *(Etc.)*

LORD MAYOR: What's the meaning of this? What's going on here?

SHAFTO: Nothing right now, sir. But within the hour Maid Marjorie and I will be married in the village church. You are all invited to the wedding.

MARIGOLD: But you promised to marry me!

MAGNOLIA: And me!

MORNING GLORY: And me!

MAID MARJORIE: Alas, Bobby, how could you do such a thing?

SHAFTO *(Taking her hands):* But I didn't, Marjorie. I made only one promise of marriage, and that promise was to you.

LADIES *(Each brandishing her letter):* But your letters!

LORD MAYOR: If you have made false promises to my daughters, you will spend the rest of your life in prison. *(To daughters)* Let me see those letters.

MAGNOLIA *(Handing her letter to* LORD MAYOR*):* Read it, Father.

LORD MAYOR *(Reading):*

    Magnolia fair, I've gone to win
    A fortune for you when my ship comes in!

MARIGOLD: Read mine, too, Father! *(She hands him her note.)*

LORD MAYOR *(Reading):*
> I promise you, dear Marigold,
> More treasure than your arms can hold!

MORNING GLORY: And this is what he wrote to *me*, Father. *(Hands him her note)*

LORD MAYOR *(Reading):*
> Dear Morning Glory, bright and fair,
> Some day my fortune you will share!

(To SHAFTO*)* Well, young man, what do you have to say for yourself?

SHAFTO: "Actions speak louder than words," Your Honor. *(Reaching into chest and producing two bags of gold which he presents to* MAGNOLIA*)*
> My ship is in, as you have heard,
> And with this gold, I keep my word!

MAGNOLIA: But, Father, he promised . . .

LORD MAYOR: And he's kept his promise, daughter, just as his letter said.

SHAFTO: And now, if my mates will give me a hand with those heavy bags, I'll keep the rest of my promises. *(Bowing to* MARIGOLD, *he gives her with two bags handed to him by* SAILORS*)*
> I promised you, dear Marigold,
> More treasure than your arms can hold!

(As he hands her a third bag, she drops one)

LORD MAYOR: Again he's kept his word! *(Picking up the bag she dropped)* He's given you more than you can carry.

SHAFTO *(Receiving two more bags from* SAILORS *and bowing before* MORNING GLORY*)*:
> Dear Morning Glory, bright and fair,
> Here is my gold for you to share!

GARDENER *(Clapping him on the shoulder):* You're a

brave lad, Bobby Shafto! And a man of honor!

SHAFTO: Thank you, sir! And now, with your permission, I will keep my promise to Maid Marjorie.

LORD MAYOR: Just a minute! Just a minute! Although you have kept your promises to my daughters, I don't understand why you made them in the first place. Why would you wish to share your fortune with Magnolia, Marigold and Morning Glory?

GARDENER: I think I can explain that, Your Honor. (Producing folded paper) Perhaps you will remember this agreement we signed when you first became Lord Mayor of Florabella.

LORD MAYOR: Agreement? What agreement?

GARDENER: A legal agreement, Your Honor. This document grants me the right to buy back my original orchards and farmlands if and when I ever have the money to do so. Since the property belongs not only to you, but to your daughters as well, Bobby Shafto has already paid them for their shares.

SHAFTO: And there's more than enough gold in that chest to meet your price.

LORD MAYOR: But what if I refuse to sell?

SHAFTO: A bargain is a bargain, sir, and a promise is a promise! I have kept mine. Now it is your turn.

MAGNOLIA: It's a trick, Father!

LORD MAYOR (Studying document, then slowly) This document is perfectly legal. And as for his promises to you, daughters, he has kept them to the letter.

MAGNOLIA (Sniffing): But he has broken my heart!

MARIGOLD (Dabbing at her eyes): And mine!

MORNING GLORY (With a sob): And mine!

LORD MAYOR: Nonsense! When you thought he was a penniless sailor lad, you turned your backs on him. Now, stop your sniffling and wish Bobby Shafto and his bride the happiness they deserve.

MAGNOLIA (*To* 1ST SAILOR): If you will relieve me of these heavy bags, I will be glad to. (*Hands bags to* 1ST SAILOR) Maid Marjorie, my apologies! Master Shafto, my congratulations!

MARIGOLD (*Handing her bags to* 2ND SAILOR): Master Shafto, it seems my sisters and I read more into your promises than you intended. Please accept my best wishes.

MORNING GLORY (*Handing her money bags to* LORD MAYOR): A long and happy life to you both!

MAID MARJORIE: Thank you! I hope you will all come to our wedding.

LORD MAYOR: With pleasure, my dear. And after the ceremony, your father and I will transact our business. Your lands will be returned to you as the contract provides.

GARDENER: Thank you, Your Honor.

LORD MAYOR: On one condition! (*Pause*) That this evening's ball be considered a wedding reception for the bride and groom.

MARJORIE *and* SHAFTO: Delighted, Your Honor.

ALL (*Singing*):
> Bobby Shafto's home from sea,
> Home to wed Maid Marjorie!
> Oh, how happy they will be,
> Hail to Bobby Shafto!

(*Curtain*)

THE END

The Mouse That Soared

Characters

ORVIE MOUSE
MAMMA MOUSE
FRISKY
WHISKERS } *the "Three Blind Mice"*
RISKY
SCAMPER, *mouse who plays the "Farmer's Wife"*
LONG TAIL
SHORT TAIL
NIBBLER
SCRIBBLER
FLUTTER } *other mice*
FURRY
SQUEAKY
SQUEALY
BILL
JANE } *students*
THOMAS CAT
ANNOUNCER, *offstage voice*

SETTING: *Merry Mouse Meadow.*
AT RISE: FRISKY, WHISKERS, *and* RISKY, *who are blindfolded, join hands and go around in a circle*

singing "Three Blind Mice." SCAMPER, *as the "Farmer's Wife," brandishes a cardboard carving knife and tries to break through circle. When they finish song, "Farmer's Wife" chases "Three Blind Mice" as they break circle and run in all directions, until she catches one. During game,* ORVIE *sits under tree, ignoring the others and pretending to read a torn scrap of newspaper. Other mice stand around stage and watch game.*

FRISKY: That was fun! Let's play again.

WHISKERS *(As he takes off blindfold):* Come on, Orvie, you play this time.

ORVIE: No, thanks. I want no part of that stupid game!

SCAMPER *(Offering* ORVIE *the carving knife):* But it's fun. Take my part.

ORVIE: No, thanks.

NIBBLER: Oh, come on, Orvie. We need your voice. You're such a good squeaker.

ORVIE: I wouldn't sing that foolish song!

SCAMPER: What's foolish about it?

ORVIE: Everything! It makes us mice look silly and stupid.

LONG TAIL *(Rubbing his head):* I never thought of that.

ORVIE: Well, think about it. Actually, mice are very clever creatures. We have to be to stay alive.

SHORT TAIL: Maybe we could play "Hickory Dickory Dock!"

ORVIE: That's almost as bad.

FURRY *(Singing in squeaky voice):*

> Hickory dickory dock,
> The mouse ran up the clock.
> The clock struck one,
> The mouse ran down.
> Hickory dickory dock!

RISKY: What's wrong with that?

ORVIE (*Impatiently*): Don't you see? The mouse was a coward. Afraid of a little old clock! He ran away.

WHISKERS: I never thought of that!

ORVIE: You're all too busy running away to think of anything. You're even afraid of old Thomas the Cat!

RISKY: Sh-h-h! Don't even mention him. He might hear you.

ORVIE: And what if he does? He's half blind and almost toothless. Yet you're all scared to death of him.

LONG TAIL: Mice are just naturally timid!

ORVIE: That's not true. Why doesn't anybody write songs about our mouse heroes?

SCRIBBLER: I don't know any mouse heroes.

ORVIE: Shame on you! What about our great ancestor who wasn't afraid of a lion?

SQUEAKY (*Jumping up and down*): Oh, I know about him. He even saved the lion's life.

ORVIE: And what about the brave mice who sailed with Columbus and the ones who came with the Pilgrims on the *Mayflower*? And take my own ancestor—Orville Mouse, the First.

SCRIBBLER: Tell us about him, Orvie. Maybe I could write a song about him.

ORVIE (*Strutting about*): He lived in the little bicycle shop where the famous Wright brothers built the first airplane. He was named for Orville Wright himself.

FURRY: How exciting!

SQUEAKY: I'll bet you would be a real mouse hero, Orvie, if you had the chance.

SQUEALY: But nothing exciting ever happens here in Merry Mouse Meadow. (*There is a loud noise offstage. All except* ORVIE *run to one side and huddle together in terror.*)

ORVIE: Cowards!

ALL *(Creeping back to center; ad lib):* What was that? What made that noise? I'm scared. *(Etc.)*

FRISKY: It sounded like the end of the world.

ORVIE: It was a rocket taking off across the field.

WHISKERS: A rocket? When? Where?

ORVIE *(Annoyed):* Don't you ever read the papers? Here, Scribbler. *(Hand him paper)* Read this.

SCRIBBLER *(Reading):* "The Junior Science Club meets every Saturday morning in Pleasant Acres, where they have built a launching pad for their rockets. The President of the Club told reporters they are planning to send up a mouse in their next experiment."

SQUEAKY *(Frightened):* Run for your lives! *(All start off.)*

ORVIE: Wait! Stop! Where are you going?

SHORT TAIL: You know they're looking for a mouse to send up in their rocket.

ORVIE: There's nothing to be afraid of. You're all perfectly safe.

SCAMPER: How do you know?

ORVIE: Because they're going to take *me.*

RISKY: You!

ORVIE: Yes, me! I am going to volunteer. *(Struts around)*

FURRY: What!

ORVIE: This is my big chance. Just think, I'll be the very first mousetronaut! My name will be in the headlines.

SCRIBBLER *(Dramatically):* "Orvie in orbit!" Yes, it has a terrific ring to it.

WHISKERS: But you might be killed!

ORVIE: Nonsense! I'll live to tell my great-grandchildren about my adventure in space.

SCAMPER: You will bring honor and glory to Mouseland.

RISKY: Do you really think you can do it, Orvie?

ORVIE: I know I can, but I will need your help.

ALL *(Ad lib):* Tell us what to do. We'll help you. How can we help? *(Etc.)*

ORVIE: First of all, I'll need special equipment.

SQUEALY: You'll need a space outfit.

NIBBLER: And a helmet.

SCRIBBLER: And gloves.

FURRY: And boots.

SQUEALY: Let's go collect everything he needs.

LONG TAIL: Come on, Orvie. You'll have to try them on for size.

ORVIE: You're really great to do this for me! *(All except* SCRIBBLER *and* NIBBLER *exit.)*

NIBBLER: Do you really think he can make it?

SCRIBBLER: Other animals have done it. Remember that monkey who went up in 1961? What was his name?

NIBBLER: His name was Enos. His picture was in all the papers.

SCRIBBLER: If a monkey can do it, so can a mouse.

NIBBLER: Sh-h-h! I hear somebody coming.

SCRIBBLER: Quick! Let's hide. (NIBBLER *and* SCRIBBLER *hide, as* BILL *and* JANE *enter.)*

JANE: Everything is set for the big test flight. All we need is our mouse.

BILL: We'll catch one. There are traps set all around the base.

JANE: But we haven't caught one yet. Mice are getting smarter every day.

BILL: Maybe we could catch a field mouse right here.

JANE: What do you think you are, Bill, a cat?

BILL: Sh-h-h! *(Pointing)* Look! Over there.

JANE: What? Where?

BILL: I thought I saw a mouse. Maybe we can sneak up on him.

JANE: We don't have time. We're due at the launching pad. Let's go. *(As* JANE *and* BILL *exit,* NIBBLER *and* SCRIBBLER *creep out.)*

NIBBLER: I hope they know what they're doing. Poor Orvie!

SCRIBBLER: Here he comes! *(Points off)* And look! His mother is with him. (ORVIE *enters, wearing space suit. He is followed by* MAMMA MOUSE *and other mice.)*

MAMMA MOUSE: Orvie, are you sure you'll be all right?

ORVIE: Of course, Mamma. Don't worry.

LONG TAIL: We'll see you off.

SCRIBBLER: No, we'd better stay here.

NIBBLER: We just found out there are mousetraps all over the base.

SCAMPER: How will we know what happens?

WHISKERS: We can listen on the radio.

FRISKY: I brought my transwhisker!

MAMMA MOUSE *(Throwing her arms around* ORVIE*):* Oh, Orvie! Orvie! I can't let you go!

ORVIE: Now, now, Mamma. Don't worry. When I come back, you'll be the proudest Mamma Mouse in all the world. Squeaky, you look after her.

SQUEAKY: I'll take good care of her, Orvie.

ORVIE: And now I must be off. Thanks for all your help.

ALL: Good luck, Orvie. (ORVIE *exits, as all wave and sing to the tune of "Good Night, Ladies.")*
Good luck, Orvie! Good luck, Orvie! Good luck, Orvie! Come back here safe and sound.

MAMMA MOUSE: I think I'm going to cry.

RISKY: Come and sit by me, and we'll listen to the radio.

(Mice form semi-circle around FRISKY, *who has radio.)*

FRISKY *(Turning dial):* It's too soon for any news.

FLUTTER: While we're waiting, I think we should plan a celebration for Orvie's return.

FURRY: We'll give him a banquet.

LONG TAIL: We'll have music and speeches.

SCRIBBLER: I've already started a poem. Listen: It's called "Ode to Orville." *(Takes paper from pocket and reads)*

> Out by the towering launching Pad
> The brave Meadow Mouse stands.
> The mouse a mighty mouse is he
> With large and lofty plans,
> And the courage of his tiny heart
> Is strong as iron bands!

(All applaud.)

SCAMPER: Let's hear the rest of it.

SCRIBBLER: That's as far as I can go till I see what happens.

WHISKERS: Turn on the radio now, Frisky. It must be close to launching time. (FRISKY *turns knob on radio. He pretends to listen closely.)*

FRISKY: I can't quite get the station, but I think they said they were starting the countdown.

ALL *(Singing to the tune of "John Brown Had A Little Indian"):*

> One little, two little, three little seconds,
> Four little, five little, six little seconds,
> Seven little, eight little, nine little seconds,
> Ten little seconds to go!
> Ten little, nine little, eight little seconds,
> Seven little, six little, five little seconds,

Four little, three little, two little seconds,
One little second to go!
(Loud crash and whistling sound from offstage. All speak ad lib.) He's off! He's off! *(They look up.)* Whee-ee! There goes Orvie! *(Etc.)*

MAMMA MOUSE *(Jumping up in a frenzy):* Orville! Orville Mouse! Come back!

SQUEAKY *(Comforting her):* There, there, Mamma Mouse.

FRISKY: Sh-h-h! I think I'm getting something on the radio. *(All crouch down and listen.)*

ANNOUNCER *(Offstage, on loudspeaker):* "A perfect take-off! Everything is going according to plan, and all precautions have been taken to bring our mouse passenger safely back to earth."

SQUEALY: Hear that, Mamma Mouse? There's nothing to worry about.

LONG TAIL: Orvie is going to be a hero for sure.

SHORT TAIL: We must give him a medal.

FLUTTER: Where will we get one?

RISKY: Let's give him Thomas Cat's bell!

WHISKERS: Thomas Cat's bell! How would we get it?

RISKY: If Orvie can be a hero, so can we! We'll take it right off Tom's neck. *(Looks around)* All in favor?

ALL: Aye! Aye!

FURRY: Sh-h-h! I think I hear the cat coming now. Quick, let's hide. *(All hide behind bushes, as* THOMAS CAT *enters.)*

THOMAS CAT: I smell something funny! Not a mouse in sight! *(Mice dash out and attack* THOMAS CAT. *In the scuffle, two of them sit on* THOMAS CAT, *as* SQUEALY *takes the bell from around his neck.)*

SQUEALY: We have it! We have the bell!

THOMAS CAT: Let me up! Let me up!

MICE: Promise to do us no harm.

THOMAS CAT: I promise. *(They let him up.)* Now what was that all about? Why did you take my bell?

NIBBLER: It's for Orvie.

SCRIBBLER: Orvie is a hero now. We want to give him a medal.

THOMAS CAT: Orvie has always been a hero. He was the only mouse who was never afraid of me. If you had told me the bell was for Orvie, I would have given it to you without all this fuss.

SCAMPER: Thanks, Thomas. Listen to the radio with us for news of Orvie's return to earth.

THOMAS CAT: We don't need the radio for that. Orvie has already landed safe and sound.

MAMMA MOUSE: How do you know?

THOMAS CAT: I've just come from the field. Orvie is in great shape.

ALL: Hurrah! Hurrah! Hurrah!

THOMAS CAT: As soon as he has his medical checkup, he'll be home.

FRISKY: Come on, everyone. We must get our band instruments and welcome Orvie home.

MICE *(Ad lib):* Yes, let's. Come on, hurry! *(Etc.)* (FRISKY, WHISKERS, FURRY, FLUTTER, SQUEAKY, *and* SQUEALY *exit.)*

THOMAS CAT *(To mice as they exit):* Bring me my fiddle. I want to take part in the celebration.

MAMMA MOUSE: Are you sure Orvie is all right?

THOMAS CAT: As right as rain, ma'am.

SCRIBBLER: Dear me. I must finish my poem. *(Takes pad of paper from pocket and begins to scribble rapidly)*

MAMMA MOUSE *(Looking offstage):* Here they come with their instruments. *(Mice return with sheets of paper and rhythm instruments, including fiddle for* THOMAS CAT.*)*

FRISKY: We're all tuned up and ready to go with "Three Blind Mice."

RISKY: But Orvie hates that song.

FLUTTER: We made up some new words, and here's a copy for each of you. *(Gives sheet to each one.)*

MAMMA MOUSE *(Looking off left):* Here he comes. *(Running to meet* ORVIE *as he enters)* Oh, Orvie, Orvie! Welcome home!

ALL *(Singing to accompaniment of rhythm instruments):*
> One brave mouse! One brave mouse!
> See how he soars! See how he soars!
> He soars right up in the morning light,
> Away he goes like a flying kite!
> Did ever you see such a wonderful sight
> As one brave mouse!

(All ad lib greetings). Welcome home, Orvie! Are you all right? Congratulations! *(Etc.)*

ORVIE: Thank you. Thank you.

SCAMPER: As a small token of our admiration, we wish to present you with this medal. *(Hangs the bell around* ORVIE'S *neck.)* May you wear it with pride and honor.

ORVIE: But this is Thomas Cat's bell. How did you get it?

THOMAS CAT: They jumped me and took it by force.

ORVIE: But they've always been scared to death of you!

SCRIBBLER: Not any more, Orvie. Some of your courage must have rubbed off on us. All we needed was a hero to look up to. Listen! *(Reads poem)*
> Our thanks to you, dear Orvie Mouse,
> For the lesson you have taught.

In your brave deed each timid mouse
Found courage that he sought.
From this day forth, we sing your praise,
O mighty mousetronaut!
(All applaud as curtain falls.)

THE END

The Gentle Giant-Killer

Characters

MISS BLANK ⎤
MISS BURTON ⎬ *owners of the Busy Bee*
MISS BROWN ⎦ *Employment Agency*
JACK
MISS GOODE, *a teacher*
MR. MASON, *a janitor*
MARY ⎤
HENRY │
SALLY │
FREDDIE │
SARA │
JILL ⎬ *children in Miss Goode's class*
BETTY │
JOHNNY │
JANE │
JOSEPH │
WILLIE ⎦

SETTING: *The Busy Bee Employment Agency. Two chairs and a desk with telephone and index card file are at one side of stage, in front of curtain.*
BEFORE RISE: MISS BLANK *enters, sits at desk.* JACK

enters, carrying attaché case. He sits in front of desk, places case beside him. She writes as he answers her questions.

MISS BLANK: Name, please.

JACK: My name is Jack.

MISS BLANK: Last name?

JACK: Blank.

MISS BLANK: What did you say?

JACK: Blank! Leave that blank.

MISS BLANK *(Angrily):* Young man, are you poking fun at me?

JACK: Of course not! What ever made you think such a thing?

MISS BLANK: Because my name is Blank. Bertha Blank.

JACK *(Rising):* How do you do, Miss Blank? Please believe me—I was not making fun of you. I merely asked you to leave a blank space for my last name, because I don't have one.

MISS BLANK: Nonsense! Everybody has a last name.

JACK *(Sitting):* Everybody but me!

MISS BLANK *(Flustered):* But I must put down something.

JACK: Put down "Something." Jack Something. I like that.

MISS BLANK: This is most irregular.

JACK: But then, I'm not a regular guy!

MISS BLANK: Now look here, Mr.—er—Mr. Something, if you really want the Busy Bee Employment Agency to find a job for you, you must cooperate!

JACK: I'll try.

MISS BLANK: Now what experience have you had?

JACK *(Blankly):* Experience?

MISS BLANK *(With exaggerated patience):* Job experience. What kind of work do you do?

JACK: I'm a giant-killer.

MISS BLANK *(Rising; angrily):* I'm warning you, sir. I will not put up with your bad jokes any longer.

JACK: But I'm not joking. I am a professional giant-killer.

MISS BLANK *(Reaching for phone):* I'm going to call the police.

JACK: They already know about me.

MISS BLANK: They do?

JACK: Certainly. I've already offered my services to the police, but they don't need a giant-killer.

MISS BLANK *(Nervously):* I—I—you'll have to excuse me. I—that is—there's something I must attend to in the other office.

JACK *(Upset):* Don't go. You don't need to be afraid of me. I wouldn't hurt a fly.

MISS BLANK: But you're a giant-killer!

JACK: An ex-giant-killer! I haven't slain a giant since the days of King Arthur.

MISS BLANK: King Arthur! Now I know you're out of your mind! I'm getting out of here!

JACK *(Blocking her way):* Please, please, Miss Blank! Let me explain!

MISS BLANK *(Frightened):* Don't try to stop me! *(Calls loudly)* Help! Help! (MISS BURTON *and* MISS BROWN *enter.*)

MISS BURTON *(Alarmed):* What's the matter, Bertha?

MISS BLANK: This—this man! He's a madman! A killer!

JACK: Please, ladies, I can explain everything!

MISS BLANK: Get him out of here! Run for your lives!

MISS BROWN: Now, now, Bertha, don't get hysterical. *(Eyeing* JACK*)* He looks like a harmless fellow.

MISS BURTON: Who are you, young man? What are you doing here?

JACK: I'm trying to get a job, and this agency was recommended to me.

MISS BURTON: What is your name?

JACK: Promise you won't panic if I tell you.

MISS BURTON: Miss Brown and I are not the panicky type.

JACK: Very well, then. I am Jack the Giant-Killer.

MISS BROWN (*Laughing*): I'll bet you are!

MISS BURTON: Jack the Giant-Killer, indeed!

MISS BLANK: He means it, girls. He's a dangerous character.

JACK: I'm nothing of the sort! Even when I was at the peak of my career, I arranged matters so that the monsters would destroy themselves.

MISS BURTON: Sit down, young man. You're beginning to interest me.

JACK (*As he and* MISS BURTON *sit down*): Thank you, Miss—er—Miss—

MISS BURTON: Miss Burton. I am the president of the employment agency. My partner, Miss Brown, is the first vice-president, and my other partner, Miss Blank, whom you have already met, is the second vice-president.

MISS BROWN: That's why we call our agency the Busy Bees—Burton, Brown, and Blank!

JACK: How clever! And I hope you can help me find a job. Please listen to me.

MISS BROWN: We've never had any calls for a giant-killer.

JACK: That's why I'm out of work. There just aren't any more giants.

MISS BURTON (*Thoughtfully*): Well, there's the jolly green fellow who grows vegetables.

MISS BLANK: But he's friendly giant. No one would want to kill him.

JACK (*Impatiently*): You still don't understand. Actually, I never liked giant killing. I went into the business only as a public service.

ALL: A public service!

JACK: Yes. Take my first giant—*(Rising)* Coromoran. I had to get rid of him because he was devouring all the crops and cattle for miles around. If he'd lived much longer, all the farmers in our area would have been ruined.

MISS BURTON: They must have been very grateful to you.

JACK: Oh, yes. They're the folks who named me Jack the Giant-Killer, and I still have the magic sword they gave me. Then the next giant, old Blunderbore, had the dungeon of his castle filled with prisoners, mostly women and children. So I did away with him, and released the victims.

MISS BURTON *(Enthusiastically):* A rescue mission!

JACK: Right! That's what I like best, rescue work. Don't you have anyone in your files who needs to be rescued?

MISS BURTON: Look through the card index, Bertha, and see what you can find. (MISS BLANK *starts to look through file.)*

MISS BROWN: Basically every "Help Wanted" notice is a plea for some kind of rescue. Hm-m-m. *(Files through cards)*

MISS BURTON: Perhaps something in the technical field. Bertha, look under the T's.

MISS BLANK *(Flipping through cards):* T . . . Tailor . . . Taxi driver . . . Taxidermist . . . Teacher . . . Wait a minute! What about the teacher who was down here yesterday? What was her name?

MISS BROWN: Miss Goode! Look under the G's.

MISS BURTON: She was a damsel in distress, if I ever saw one.

JACK: What was her trouble?

MISS BURTON: The children! All twenty-three of them.

(NOTE: *Use number of children in participating class.*)

MISS BLANK: But you wouldn't want that job!

JACK: Why not? I love children.

MISS BLANK *(Taking card from file):* Not these children! Listen to this: *(Reads)* "*Wanted:* Assistant English Teacher to instruct children who are careless, exasperating, forgetful, giggly, impolite, jittery, lazy, mischievous, naughty, pesky, rude, slangy, troublesome, ungrammatical, wiggly, yawny, and zany!"

JACK *(Leaping to his feet):* There must be a giant loose in that school room.

MISS BURTON: What are you talking about?

JACK: Only a giant could weave such a spell over innocent children! I must rescue them at once.

MISS BURTON: This is not the age of knighthood, Jack.

JACK: Nevertheless, I smell a giant!

Fee, Fie, Fo, Fum!

I smell the blood of a giant, by gum!

And, furthermore, I think I know who it is!

(Opens his attaché case)

MISS BLANK: What are you doing?

JACK *(Taking out a pointed cap, a sword, a cloak and a pair of fancy bedroom slippers):* Getting my equipment ready.

MISS BROWN: But you don't even know where the school is!

JACK *(Putting on cap):* I do now! This is my Know-It-All cap—I captured it from a two-headed giant in Wales. *(Listening)* Aha! I was right! Ladies, my cap has not only given me the location of the school, but it has also confirmed my suspicions! This giant is Blunderbore the Second, son of Blunderbore the First, whom I killed. He was only a baby when I came to his father's castle, so I spared his life. I should have known he'd cause trouble. *(He changes his shoes for bedroom slippers.)*

MISS BURTON: Why are you changing your shoes?

JACK: These are my magic slippers. They will take me anywhere I want to go, as swiftly as the wind. *(Buckling on his sword)* And with this magic sword I will slay that wicked Blunderbore and set those children free! *(Drawing sword and striking a pose)*

> I swear before I go to bed,
> I'll grind his bones to make my bread!

(All exit)

* * *

SETTING: *Miss Goode's classroom. At one side of room is a large screen with names of parts of speech on the front. A pile of straw is hidden behind it.*

AT RISE: MARY, HENRY, SALLY, FREDDIE, SARA, JILL, BETTY, JOHNNY, JANE, JOSEPH, *and* WILLIE *are sitting at desks, wiggling, giggling, stretching, yawning, and dozing.* MISS GOODE *sits at her desk, trying to get their attention.*

MISS GOODE: Now, please, children, let me have your attention.

WILLIE: We don't have any! We gave you our attention yesterday, and you never gave it back!

MISS GOODE: Willie Jones, you are impudent! Sara, sit up! Johnny, sit still! Henry, wake up! Freddie, stop yawning!

FREDDIE: But I'm so bored! *(Yawning)* Ho-hum!

MISS GOODE *(Sternly):* Boys and girls, listen to me. Now, we are going to review the parts of speech.

SARA: What parts of speech?

MISS GOODE: You know perfectly well, Sara. (*To* JANE) Jane, what is a noun?

JANE: I can't remember, Miss Goode.

MISS GOODE (*Impatiently*): How could you forget when we've been going over these definitions all week? Now get out your notebooks, children, and we'll go over them once more.

JOSEPH (*As children look through desks for notebooks*): I can't find mine, Miss Goode.

MISS GOODE: Joseph Jennings, don't tell me you left yours at home again!

JOSEPH: I don't know where I left it.

MISS GOODE: Carelessness! Carelessness! Carelessness! (*There is a knock at the door right, and* JACK *looks in.*)

JACK: Excuse me, Miss Goode. May I come in?

MISS GOODE: I'm sorry, but this is not a visiting day.

JACK (*Entering*): But I am not a visitor. I am the assistant you requested. The Busy Bee Employment Agency sent me.

MISS GOODE: Oh, do come in, sir, and let me introduce you to the children. Boys and girls, this is Mr.—Mr.—

JACK: Mr. Jack.

ALL: Good morning, Mr. Jack.

JACK: And good morning to you! My, oh, my! What a bright, handsome, intelligent, lively group of children!

ALL (*Straightening up and smiling*): Thank you, Mr. Jack.

JACK: And so polite, too!

MISS GOODE: I'm glad you find them so cooperative, Mr. Jack.

JACK: But naturally. I expect them to be cooperative . . . also alert, busy, careful. . . .

HENRY: But we're really not like that at all, sir. Usually
we are . . .

ALL *(Ad lib):* Careless, exasperating, forgetful, lazy . . .
(Etc.)

JACK: So I've heard. But I know it can't be true.

JOHNNY: Oh, but it is!

MARY: We don't really want to be lazy, mischievous,
naughty, or noisy . . .

SALLY: We try not to be pesky, rude, or slangy. . . .

FREDDIE: But no matter how hard we try, we always end
up being terribly troublesome and ungrammatical.

JACK: That's the whole trouble. You're ungrammatical,
so you say the wrong words, and seem much worse
than you really are.

MISS GOODE: I've tried and tried to teach them good
grammar, but they haven't learned a thing!

MARY *(Sadly):*
Our subjects and verbs! Oh, they never agree!
We *know* "It is I," but we *say* "It is me"!

HENRY:
"He don't" is all wrong, and "He *doesn't*" is right,
But we never remember from morning till night!

SALLY:
And verbs are so hard, we're ready to scream
With *take, took,* and *taken,* and *see, saw,* and *seen!*

WILLIE:
And when to say *lie* and when to say *lay,*

SARA:
And when to say *can* and when to say *may!*

FREDDIE:
And when to say *let* and when to say *leave,*

BETTY:
Does "i" follow "e" when you're spelling *receive?*

JOHNNY:

> You speak of a *house*, and two of them—*houses;*
> You speak of a *mouse*, but two are not *mouses!*

JANE:

> More than one *goose* turns out to be *geese*,
> But more than one *moose* is not ever *meese!*

JOSEPH:

> Oh, grammar is ghastly! It doesn't make sense!
> All mixed up with clauses and pronouns and tense!

JILL:

> When you open your mouth, you're breaking a rule!

ALL:

> And that is why grammar should not be in school!

MISS GOODE: You see, Mr. Jack, that teaching grammar is a hopeless task.

JACK: The children are not to blame, Miss Goode, and neither are you. It's old Blunderbore the Giant who has you in his power!

BETTY: Blunderbore? Who's he?

JACK: Shh! Not so loud! He might hear you! *(Looks about suspiciously)*

> Old Blunderbore is a terrible fellow
> With two big heads and a horrible bellow!
> And once he has you in his grip,
> He makes you stumble, he makes you slip!
> He makes you blunder, and what is more,
> He makes your lessons a terrible bore!
> He takes all the fun out of study, and worse—
> He makes you feel that reading's a curse!
> He makes you look stupid and lazy, too,
> You make mistakes in whatever you do.
> You can put it down as a general rule,

When children hate to go to school,
And mumble and grumble and moan and howl,
Old Blunderbore is on the prowl!

SARA *(A little frightened):* Oh, dear, Mr. Jack, do you think he's here now?

JACK: I'm positive.

WILLIE: But where?

JACK: He could be anywhere. *(Drawing his sword and pointing)* Maybe he's up there in the light fixture. *(All look up.)*

JOHNNY: A giant couldn't get into a light fixture!

JACK: Blunderbore could. He gets little or big.

MARY: But I don't see him.

JACK: No doubt he's wearing his invisible cloak. Maybe he's behind the bookcase. *(Looks behind bookcase)* No! Not there! *(Loud roaring and banging is heard offstage.)* Hear that? He's coming! Quick! Hide behind your desks! *(Children crouch.)* You, too, Miss Goode. Get behind your desk. *(Noise increases)* Now, don't be afraid. I won't let him hurt you!

MISS GOODE: Nonsense! We often hear that noise. It's the heat coming in from the radiators.

JACK: That's what you may think, Miss Goode, but I know better. It's Blunderbore himself, and he's coming this way! Now get behind that desk and stay there till I sound the all-clear. Hurry! *(She squats down.)* Here he comes, heading right for the grammar display! *(*JACK* goes behind screen; grunts and groans are heard.)* Aha, you wretch! This time you have *me* to reckon with! *(Struggling noises and groans are heard.)* Take that! And that! *(More noises)* And that! And that! *(Shouts and groans stop.* JACK *calls from behind screen.)* All clear! Old Blunderbore is dead!

(MISS GOODE *and children jump up, remove screen, and reveal* JACK, *standing with his sword aloft and his foot firmly planted on a pile of straw.*)

ALL *(Ad lib):* Where is he? Where's the giant? We can't see him. *(Etc.)*

JACK *(Pointing with his sword to a pile of straw):* Right there in front of you. At least that's all that's left of him!

FREDDIE: But that's only a pile of straw.

JOHNNY: I'd say you really knocked the stuffing out of him!

SARA: But if he was only made of straw, we could have destroyed him ourselves.

JACK: Oh, no! He turned to straw only after I killed him. You were under his wicked spell. But, now, you are free!

JACK: By making the most of your freedom and learning those parts of speech the easy way.

MARY: Is there an easy way?

JACK: There's an easy way to do most everything, young lady, if you take the trouble to find the formula.

MISS GOODE: Formula? What formula?

JACK *(Looking around):* It should be here somewhere. (MR. MASON *enters carrying a long-handled mop.*)

MR. MASON: What's going on here? All that crashing and banging! And what's this dirty straw doing on my nice, clean floor?

HENRY: That's a giant! At least it *was* a giant.

MR. MASON: A giant! It looks more like one of those silly projects to me! Sorry, Miss Goode, I don't mean to criticize, but sometimes those projects are pretty messy.

MISS GOODE: It's hard to explain, Mr. Mason, but I can assure you it won't happen again.

MR. MASON: I'll just sweep it into the hall, if you're sure you've finished with it.

MISS GOODE (As MR. MASON *sweeps):* Yes, Mr. Mason, and thank you. (JACK *leans over and picks up a thick envelope from under straw.*)

JACK: Oho! Here it is! I knew it must be here somewhere.

MISS GOODE (As JACK *hands her the envelope*): What is it?

JACK: The formula for learning those parts of speech the easy way.

SALLY: Open it! Open it!

JACK *(Holding up his hand):* It's for you to open after I've gone.

MISS GOODE: Can't you stay with us for a while?

JACK: Sorry, but I have work to do. Now that I'm back in the business of giant-killing, I must keep right on the job.

JANE: Are there more giants?

JACK: I'm afraid so. Blunderbore the Second had plenty of relatives. There was his twin brother, Bungle-Brain, and I seem to remember some other relatives, Muddle-Mind and Knuckle-Head. I'd better go back to the Busy Bee Agency and see if they've had any more calls from distressed teachers.

MISS GOODE: Just the other day our math teacher, Miss Minus, was complaining about her class.

JACK: A sure sign that another giant is on the loose. Well, goodbye, Miss Goode. It's been a pleasure to help you. Goodbye, boys and girls.

ALL: Goodbye, Mr. Jack. *(He exits.)*

JILL: Aren't you going to open the envelope, Miss Goode?

MISS GOODE: Right this minute, Jill. *(She opens enve-*

lope, takes out a sheaf of song sheets and a letter.)

JOSEPH: What's in it?

MISS GOODE: Some song sheets and a letter. I'll read it to you. It's headed THE MAGIC FORMULA. *(Reading)*
> "When study is hard and learning is slow,
> Here is a secret it pays you to know:
> Just fit the subject to a song
> And sing the verses loud and long.
> And when you know the words and tune,
> You'll learn your lessons very soon."

BETTY: It sounds like fun.

WILLIE: Let's try it.

MISS GOODE *(As she distributes song sheets)*: Here are the words, and the tune is one we all know—"*Do, Re, Mi.*" (MISS GOODE *leads class in the song.)*

ALL *(Singing):*
> *Go*—a *Verb*, an action verb,
> *Noun*—a person, place or thing,
> *Me*—a *Pronoun* for my name,
> *Prepositions* phrases bring!
> *Adjectives* can all describe,
> *Adverbs* tell how, where, and when,
> *And* and *But* connect the tribe
> Of words we sing again.
> Oh, oh, oh—

(Children repeat song, with MISS GOODE *giving the command before each line.)*

MISS GOODE: Verbs!

CHILDREN *(Singing):*
> *Go* and *come* or *walk* and *run!*

MISS GOODE: Nouns!

CHILDREN *(Singing):*
> *Town* and *country, land* and *air!*

MISS GOODE: Adjectives!

CHILDREN *(Singing)*:
    Big and *small* or *short* or *tall!*
MISS GOODE: Adverbs!
CHILDREN *(Singing)*:
    Now and *then* and *here* and *there!*
MISS GOODE: Prepositions!
CHILDREN *(Singing)*:
    In and *out* and *by* and *for!*
MISS GOODE: Pronouns!
CHILDREN *(Singing)*:
    You and *I* and *everyone!*
MISS GOODE: Conjunctions!
CHILDREN *(Singing)*:
    And and *but* and *either, or!*
    The Parts of Speech are fun!
    (Curtain)

THE END

Simple Simon's Reward

Characters

Simple Simon
Patty
Pieman, *her father*
Countess of Scrubsville
Lord Scrub-A-Dub
Herald
Bob
Fred
Jack
Dick
Lady
Gentleman
Woman
Two Children
Three Girls

SETTING: *Road to fairground. An open booth is at center, with many pies on counter, and sign reading* PIES FOR SALE *tacked to edge. Several tables with chairs and benches are left and right of booth.*
AT RISE: PATTY *stands in booth, waving flyswatter over pies.*

116

PATTY *(Singing):*
　　　　Shoo fly, don't bother me,
　　　　Shoo fly, don't bother me,
　　　　Shoo fly, don't bother me,
　　　　For I belong to somebody!

SIMON *(Entering left):* Hello, Patty, how's business?

PATTY: Terrible, Simon! Simply terrible! I haven't sold a pie all morning.

SIMON *(Sniffing):* Um-m-m! They look delicious!

PATTY: Want one? Someone might as well enjoy them.

SIMON *(Shaking his head):* I don't have a cent.

PATTY: That doesn't matter. What will you have—apple or cherry?

SIMON: Neither, Patty. Thanks just the same. Your father wouldn't like me to take one without paying.

PATTY: Oh, he wouldn't care, and besides, he's not here. He went back to the bakery for more pies. He seems to think we'll do a big business today. (PATTY's *father, the* PIEMAN *enters left, pushing cart loaded with pies.*)

PIEMAN *(Calling):* Pies for sale! Fresh pies for sale! A penny a pie! *(To* PATTY*)* How is business here, Patty?

PATTY: I haven't sold a pie yet, Father.

PIEMAN *(To* SIMON*)*: Oh, hello, Simon. Want a free sample of my delicious pies?

SIMON: No, thank you, sir. I'm on my way to the fair to try to earn some money. But when I come back, I'm going to buy one of each flavor. Save some for me.

PIEMAN *(Looking at booth):* At the rate we're going now, there will be plenty left. (BOB, DICK, FRED, *and* JACK *enter left.*)

PATTY: Here are some customers now.

SIMON *(Nervously):* I don't want those boys to see me here. *(Runs and hides behind booth)*

DICK: Hello, Patty! Good morning, Pieman.

PATTY: Hello, boys. How about a nice, fresh, juicy pie?

PIEMAN *(Hopefully):* Only a penny each!

FRED: That's cheap enough! *(Reaching into pocket)* I'll take a raspberry tart.

BOB *(Impatiently):* Not now! There isn't time. Let's go!

PIEMAN: Prices will be much higher inside the fairground.

JACK: Maybe so, but we're in a hurry. Come on, Fred.

FRED: Sorry, Patty. How about coming with us to the fair?

PATTY: Thanks, but I have to help my father. (SIMON *steps out from behind booth.*)

SIMON: I'll tend the stand for you, Patty, if you want to go.

BOB: Well! If it isn't Simple Simon!

SIMON *(Furiously):* Don't you dare call me that!

BOYS *(Laughing and chanting mockingly):*
Simple Simon met a pieman going to the fair.

PATTY: Stop it! Stop it!

BOYS *(Continuing):*
Says Simple Simon to the pieman,
"Let me taste your ware."

PIEMAN: That's enough, boys.

JACK: He was too simple to know that pies cost money.

PIEMAN: Simon was only a small boy then.

PATTY: Too young to understand about money. So stop shouting that silly rhyme.

DICK: But he was old enough to know better last summer, when he went fishing in his mother's pail.

BOYS *(Mockingly):*
Simple Simon went a-fishing for to catch a whale;
All the water he had got was in his mother's pail.

BOB: How simple can you be?

SIMON: It was *not* simple!

FRED: Not simple to go fishing in a pail?

SIMON: I wasn't fishing! I was conducting an experiment.

JACK *(Laughing):* An experiment!

DICK: What kind of experiment?

SIMON: You wouldn't understand.

JACK: And were you conducting another experiment when you went looking for plums on thistles?

BOB *(Chanting):*
Simple Simon went to look if plums grew on a thistle!

FRED *(Continuing):*
He pricked his fingers very much,
which made poor Simon whistle!

SIMON: I was *not* looking for plums! I was looking for thistle flowers. They're called *plumes*, not plums!

DICK: You'll have to think of a better story than that, Simple Simon.

PIEMAN: Stop this! I won't have you teasing a customer.

BOB *(Laughing):* Simple Simon a customer?

PATTY: Yes, a customer! And one of our very best! *(Hands SIMON a pie)* Here, Simon, here is your pie. I hope you enjoy it.

FRED: Better make him show you his penny.

PIEMAN *(Sternly):* I told you boys once—that's enough! Now clear out of here!

BOB: We were only teasing, sir.

DICK: We'll go, but you'll find out for yourself just how simple Simon really is. *(To boys)* Let's go. *(Boys exit.)*

SIMON: Thanks for standing up for me, Pieman.

PIEMAN: I don't approve of name-calling. I can still remember how the boys called me pie-face when I was about your age.

PATTY: Simon, you haven't eaten your pie.

SIMON *(Returning pie to counter):* Thanks, Patty, but I don't want it unless I can pay for it.

PIEMAN: If you really feel that way about it, why not stay here and work for me?

SIMON: I'd like to, but you don't have any customers, Mr. Pastry.

PATTY (Looking off left): Yes, we do. Look! A lady and gentleman are heading this way. (LADY and GENTLEMAN enter left.)

SIMON (With a bow): Good morning, ma'am. Good morning, sir. How about a freshly-baked pie to eat at the fair?

GENTLEMAN: Sorry, boy. Pie doesn't agree with me. Always gives me indigestion.

SIMON: Perhaps the lady . . .

LADY: No, indeed! No pie for me. I'm on a diet! (LADY and GENTLEMAN exit right.)

SIMON: I'm afraid I'm not much of a salesman. (THREE GIRLS enter left.)

1ST GIRL (Approaching booth): What gorgeous pies!

2ND GIRL: What kind do you have, Mr. Pieman? (The following speeches may be sung to the tune of Buttercup's song in H.M.S. Pinafore, "I've snuff and tabachy . . .")

PIEMAN:
>I've apple and cherry,
>And lemon and berry,
>And custard with cream on the top!

SIMON:
>Your money's not wasted,
>For once you have tasted,
>You'll never be able to stop!

PATTY:
>There's pumpkin and mince pie,
>And peach pie and quince pie,
>And all of 'em baked fresh today!

PIEMAN:
> I've rhubarb and raisin,
> And what is amazin',

ALL THREE:
> There's only a penny to pay!

1ST GIRL: What do you think, girls?

2ND GIRL: We'd better wait till we come back.

3RD GIRL *(As they exit right):* We'll try not to spend all our money.

SIMON: There must be a way to get these folks to buy.

PIEMAN: If you think of something, lad, I'll make you a partner in the business.

SIMON: I have it! Why don't we move the booth inside the fairground? That's where people are spending their money.

PATTY: We don't have a permit.

PIEMAN: And we can't get one.

SIMON: Why not?

PATTY: Because, long before I was born, our family sold pies at the fair until one day, the old Duchess of Cleanser broke a tooth on a cherry pit in one of our pies. Every year since then, our request for a permit has been denied.

SIMON: But the Duchess of Cleanser died years ago.

PATTY: Yes, but her granddaughter, the Countess of Scrubsville, is even worse with her health inspections. If she ever found a speck of dirt in the bakery, I think she'd put us out of business for good.

SIMON: She'll never find any dirt in your bakery.

PIEMAN: We try to keep it clean, but the Countess is never satisfied.

SIMON: What about Lord Scrub-a-Dub? Doesn't he issue town permits and licenses?

PATTY: The Countess has Lord Scrub-a-Dub under her

thumb. (HERALD *enters left, carrying a long staff.*)

HERALD *(Loudly):* Make way for the Countess of Scrubsville and Lord Scrub-a-Dub! Make way! Make way!

PIEMAN: Quick, Patty! Cover the pies! (SIMON *helps* PATTY *spread a cloth over pies on counter, as* PIEMAN *covers those on cart.* HERALD *moves right, as* COUNTESS *and* LORD SCRUB-A-DUB, *who has a thick beard, enter left.* LORD *points to booth, and whispers to* COUNTESS. *They approach booth.*)

COUNTESS: Ah, I see you have set up your stand as close as possible to the fairground, Pieman.

PIEMAN *(Bowing):* Well within the law, milady.

COUNTESS *(With irritation):* Passable! Passable!

LORD SCRUB-A-DUB *(Inspecting booth):* You have done well to protect your pies from dust and dirt.

COUNTESS *(Running her finger along the counter):* But what is this? Something sticky!

SIMON *(Wiping the counter with his handkerchief):* That was my fault, Countess. I must have spilled some cherry juice.

COUNTESS: Indeed! And who are you? What are you doing here?

SIMON: My name is Simon, ma'am.

COUNTESS *(Thoughtfully):* Simon . . . Simon . . . I've heard that name before.

PATTY: Simon is our new helper, Countess.

COUNTESS *(To* SIMON): In that case, let me see your hands. *(Inspecting them)* They appear to be clean enough. Now let me see your nails. *(Inspecting)* Hmm-m-m! Lord Scrub-A-Dub, what do you think?

LORD SCRUB-A-DUB *(Joining her):* I agree. His hands are quite clean.

SIMON *(Pleading):* Please, Countess, please, I beg of

you to grant me a favor.

COUNTESS: Speak up, lad. What it is?

SIMON: Grant Mr. Pieman a permit to sell his pies inside the fairground.

LORD SCRUB-A-DUB *(Angrily):* What kind of simpleton are you to make such a request?

COUNTESS: Simpleton! Now I know where I heard that name before! You must be the Simple Simon I hear the children mocking in the village.

PATTY: But he is *not* simple, milady! Really, he isn't!

COUNTESS: He's worse than simple to ask such a favor. Never, never, never will I forget what happened to my beloved grandmother when she ate one of your dreadful pies and broke a tooth!

SIMON: These pies are not dreadful, milady! They're delicious!

LORD SCRUB-A-DUB *(Haughtily):* Silence! How dare you argue with the Countess?

COUNTESS: What impudence! *(Putting her hand to the side of her head)* It gives me a headache to listen to him! *(She screams.)*

LORD SCRUB-A-DUB: What is it, my dear? Do you feel faint?

COUNTESS: My earring! My diamond earring! It's gone!

LORD SCRUB-A-DUB: It can't be!

COUNTESS *(Frantically):* I've lost it! It's worth a fortune! *(Shaking her skirt)* We must find it.

LORD SCRUB-A-DUB *(Searching ground on hands and knees):* Now, don't upset yourself, my dear. We'll find it. (PATTY *searches counter;* PIEMAN *inspects the ground.)*

SIMON: Maybe you weren't wearing both earrings today, Countess.

COUNTESS: *Simple* Simon is a good name for you! I know

I was wearing both of them when I left the palace.

LORD SCRUB-A-DUB *(Rising from hands and knees):* We will offer a reward. The more searchers we have, the sooner we'll find it. *(To* HERALD*)* Herald, proclaim the news of the lost earring, and offer a one hundred pound reward for its return.

COUNTESS *(Impatiently):* There's no time to lose! (COUNTESS *and* LORD *exit left.*)

HERALD *(Striding up and down):* Hear ye! Hear ye! The Countess of Scrubsville has lost her diamond earring and offers one hundred pounds to anyone who finds it. *(Moves off right, repeating same announcement)*

PIEMAN *(Standing):* Trouble and more trouble!

SIMON: Maybe not, sir. Maybe this is the stroke of good luck we've been waiting for.

PATTY: We'll never be lucky enough to find that earring.

SIMON: Perhaps it fell into one of your pies.

PATTY *and* PIEMAN: Impossible!

SIMON: Maybe the Countess lost it while she was inspecting your bakery this morning.

PIEMAN: But my wife would have seen it.

SIMON: Not if it fell into the sugar, or the flour, or even into a kettle of custard cooking on the stove.

PIEMAN: That would ruin us forever! (WOMAN *enters right with* TWO CHILDREN.)

WOMAN *(To* CHILDREN*)*: You heard what the herald said. A hundred pound reward for that diamond earring. Now look sharp! Keep your eyes open.

SIMON: Quick, Patty! A pie! *(He bites into tart she hands him and offers a second tart to* WOMAN.*)* Would you care for a pie, ma'am?

WOMAN: This is no time for pie. We're looking for a diamond earring!

SIMON *(Still eating):* So am I, ma'am! So am I.

1ST CHILD *(Laughing)*: Isn't that just like Simple Simon?

2ND CHILD *(Mockingly)*: Looking for an earring in a pie!

SIMON: Maybe I'm not so simple, after all. It so happens the Countess was inspecting Mr. Pieman's bakery early this morning, so if she lost her earring there . . .

WOMAN: Ridiculous!

PATTY: But if it dropped into a bag of sugar . . . or a sack of flour . . . no one would have noticed.

WOMAN: What an idea! But it could be possible. *(To* PATTY) I'll take six of those pies right away.

PATTY: What kind would you like? We have apple, cherry, custard. . . .

WOMAN *(Hastily)*: Any kind. It doesn't matter. *(She takes six tarts from counter, gives two each to* CHILDREN, *then takes coins from her pocket and gives them to* PATTY.) Here you are.

PIEMAN: You may sit here and eat *(Indicating tables)*, if you wish.

WOMAN *(Sitting at table with* CHILDREN): Now be sure to eat slowly and carefully. Chew every mouthful! (BOB, DICK, FRED *and* JACK *enter right.*)

BOB: Have you heard the news, Patty?

DICK: The Countess of Scrubsville is offering a hundred pounds to anyone who finds her diamond earring.

FRED: We're off to look for it!

JACK: Want to come along?

PATTY: No, thank you. *(Biting into a tart)* We're conducting our own search right here.

PIEMAN: The Countess was in our shop this morning, and Simon says . . .

BOB: Don't tell me you'd listen to Simple Simon.

SIMON *(Taking a tart from cart)*: You won't think I'm so simple if you bite into a pie and find the missing earring. After all, the Countess was snooping about in the bakery this morning, just before these pies were baked.

BOB: That's a great idea, fellows!

PATTY: You'd better hurry before someone else finds the earring. (*Indicating* WOMAN *and* CHILDREN) Those people have already bought six pies.

FRED: We'll take six more! (*He gives her money and takes tarts from counter.*)

JACK: Make it twelve! We can easily eat three apiece. (*Pays her and takes pies. Boys sit at table, as* LADY, GENTLEMAN, *and* THREE GIRLS *enter right.*)

LADY: I can't go another step! My feet are killing me.

GENTLEMAN: But think of the reward! One hundred pounds!

SIMON: Excuse me, sir, but all of these folks are buying pies because they think the Countess may have dropped her earring at the bakery this morning. It may have fallen into the flour or the sugar. (*He bites his pie carefully.*)

GENTLEMAN: What an amazing possibility! Quick! Quick! Let me have six of those pies at once! (PATTY *and* PIEMAN *give him pies and take money.*)

LADY: At last I can sit down! (LADY *and* GENTLEMAN *sit.*)

1ST GIRL (*Eagerly*): And I'll take three! Any flavor will do!

2ND GIRL: Give me four . . . all custard! They're easier to eat.

3RD GIRL: Three for me, if you have any left.

PIEMAN (*Giving them pies and taking money*): We have only a few pies left. (HERALD *enters right, wiping his brow.*)

SIMON (*To* HERALD): How about a pie, sir? You must be

tired and hungry by now.

PATTY *(Handing* HERALD *a pie):* Do have a pie, sir! You may be the lucky one to find the earring.

HERALD: Find the earring? How could an earring be in a pie?

SIMON: Let me explain. (*He whispers into* HERALD's *ear as* COUNTESS *and* LORD SCRUB-A-DUB *enter left.*)

COUNTESS: Look at that! All those lazy, greedy people, stuffing themselves on pie, when they should be looking for my earring. (*Seeing* HERALD) Even my own servant!

HERALD *(Swallowing hard):* But, milady . . .

LORD SCRUB-A-DUB: Eating on duty! I'll deal with you when we get back to the palace.

HERALD: Please, sir, it's my duty to eat, sir. (*Pointing to* SIMON) This lad just whispered to me that the Countess dropped her earring at the bakery, and it was baked into a pie.

COUNTESS *(To* SIMON; *indignantly):* How dare you!

SIMON: I swear to you, Countess, I merely suggested that such a thing might have happened.

PIEMAN: After all, you *were* looking into our kettles!

COUNTESS: Oh, Lord Scrub-a-Dub, do you really think it's possible?

LORD SCRUB-A-DUB: Possible? It's highly possible! Pieman, hand over the rest of those pies.

SIMON: Please, sir, there is no need to look further. The earring has been found.

ALL *(Ad lib):* Found! The earring! Where? *(Etc.)*

COUNTESS: Who found it? Where is it?

LORD SCRUB-A-DUB: Why has it not been returned?

SIMON: In a moment, sir. You see, milady, I am the one who found it.

ALL: You!

COUNTESS: Then give it to me at once!

LORD SCRUB-A-DUB *(Opening purse):* I am quite prepared to pay the hundred pounds we offered as a reward.

SIMON: Oh, no, sir. It's not that. I could never accept the reward.

COUNTESS *(Haughtily):* Why not, may I ask?

SIMON: Because the earring was never *lost!*

LORD SCRUB-A-DUB: How could you find it, if it was never lost?

COUNTESS *(Impatiently):* Young man, I order you to return that earring at once!

SIMON: Perhaps Lord Scrub-a-Dub will oblige you.

LORD SCRUB-A-DUB *(Astonished):* What are you talking about?

SIMON: About the earring, Lord Scrub-a-Dub. It is in your possession.

COUNTESS: How dare you imply that Lord Scrub-a-Dub is a thief?

SIMON: I didn't say he was a thief, Countess. I merely said he has your earring.

LORD SCRUB-A-DUB: It's a lie! A lie!

SIMON: I never lie, sir. And if you will examine your beard carefully, you will find I speak the truth. (LORD SCRUB-A-DUB *runs his fingers through his beard, pulls out the earring.)*

LORD SCRUB-A-DUB *(Displaying earring):* By Jove! The boy is right!

COUNTESS: My earring! To think it was there all the time!

LORD SCRUB-A-DUB: It must have caught in my beard when I whispered to you earlier. *(To* SIMON) You are a sharp lad to notice it.

COUNTESS: You shall be rewarded for your cleverness.

GENTLEMAN *(Rising and advancing):* He deserves no reward. He is a trickster! A cheat!

WOMAN: He tricked us into buying all these pies!

BOB: He knew all the time where to find the earring!

SIMON: No! I just noticed it when the diamond glittered in the sun.

WOMAN: I don't believe you. I'm onto your salesman's tricks.

PIEMAN: If you insist that we tricked you, I will refund your money.

PATTY: Oh, no, Father! They bought the pies of their own free will, and from the way they gobbled them up, I'm sure they enjoyed every bite.

LADY: So we did, my dear. The pies were delicious. Far better than any I have ever eaten at the fair. Don't you agree, Countess?

COUNTESS: I've never tasted them.

HERALD: In that case, milady, I invite you and Lord Scrub-a-Dub to be my guests. *(Offering each a pie)* The pastry melts in your mouth, and the filling is divine.

COUNTESS *(Stepping back):* No, no, thank you! I couldn't, really!

LORD SCRUB-A-DUB: But they look so good! Indeed, I am almost tempted. . . .

SIMON: Please, milady. You offered to reward me for the return of your earring. Let this be my reward. Just taste one of the pies.

LORD SCRUB-A-DUB: Fair enough, my dear! The lad has earned the reward.

COUNTESS *(Reluctantly):* Very well. *(To* HERALD*)* We accept your offer. *(All watch anxiously as* COUNTESS

and LORD SCRUB-A-DUB *taste the pies.)* Um-m-m!
Marvelous! Marvelous! I had no idea a pie could be so
delicious!

LORD SCRUB-A-DUB: I agree. It would be a crime to
deprive the fair-goers of such a treat.

COUNTESS: Quite right! Pieman, from this day forth you
may sell your pies on the fairground.

ALL *(Cheering):* Hooray! Hooray!

LORD SCRUB-A-DUB: But what about your grandmother,
the Duchess of Cleanser, and her tooth?

COUNTESS: Breaking a tooth was well worth the price.
And from what I have seen of Mr. Pieman's bakery, I
am sure there will be no more cherry pits in his pies.

PIEMAN: Oh, thank you, thank you, milady!

COUNTESS: Don't thank me. Thank *Sir* Simon.

ALL: *Sir* Simon?

COUNTESS: That's what I said. *(To* SIMON) Kneel, Sir
Simon, and assume your rightful place as a knight of
the realm. *(He kneels and she taps him on each shoulder.)*

SIMON *(Rising):* Thank you, milady.

FRED: Just imagine! Simple Simon, a knight!

COUNTESS *(Angrily):* No more of that! Never call him by
that name again! *(To* HERALD) Herald, make a note!
The name of Simple Simon may not be used henceforth
under penalty of law!

LORD SCRUB-A-DUB: Come, Countess. We must not
keep the people at the fair waiting. (HERALD *leads the
way as* COUNTESS *and* LORD SCRUB-A-DUB *exit
right.)*

JACK: How will we ever remember? We've said that
rhyme so often, it's bound to slip out.

PIEMAN: Then learn a new one to take its place.

BOB: A new rhyme about Simon?

PIEMAN *(Reciting):* How would this be?
> Once Sir Simon met a pieman going to the fair.
> Said *Clever* Simon to the pieman, "Let me taste
> your ware!"
> The pieman said to Clever Simon, "You'll never
> need a penny!
> You eat your fill, and free of charge, as long as
> I have any!"

(All recite verse as PIEMAN, *with a flourish and a bow, gives* SIMON *a pie. Curtain)*

THE END

Shirley Holmes and the FBI

Characters

SHIRLEY HOLMES
DONNA ⎫
KATE ⎬ *her friends*
JEN ⎪
CANDY ⎭
JERRY MASON
BRUCE ⎫
LARRY ⎬ *his friends*
ALF ⎪
ADAM ⎭
BABY FACE BOYD
CURLY SMITH
OFFICER HIGGINS
OFFICER RYAN
RADIO ANNOUNCER, *offstage voice*

SETTING: *An abandoned garage. Walls are of gray cinder blocks. Door is at right. Workbench, center, is piled high with boxes, old radio, hot plate, etc. A cupboard is hidden in left corner, behind ladders, volleyball net, and canvas tarpaulin. Canvas bag,*

coffee can, and ledger book are inside cupboard. Tennis racket, baseball bat, canoe paddle, and other pieces of sports equipment are scattered around stage.
AT RISE: *The stage is dark. Then,* BABY FACE BOYD *and* CURLY SMITH *enter, shining flashlights around the walls. They wear half masks.*
BABY FACE: The loot must be here someplace, Curly.
CURLY *(Sarcastically):* Oh, sure, Baby Face! All we have to do is find it.
BABY FACE: That shouldn't be too hard. We have Gentleman Joe's directions.
CURLY: But the cops must've gone over every inch of this garage.
BABY FACE: Gentleman Joe made sure there were no clues to connect this hideaway with the Fairview holdup. After all, he was five miles outside of town when they caught him. Now, let's get moving before they send out a general alarm on our escape.
CURLY: It's so dark in here. There must be a light switch somewhere. *(He gropes along walls and door frame for switch.)*
BABY FACE: What do you expect in a garage with no windows? (CURLY *flips switch and lights go on.*) Let's have a look at those instructions. *(They turn off flashlights and put them in their pockets.)*
CURLY *(Spreading out sheet with directions on workbench):* This is Greek to me. Why couldn't he have told you straight out where he hid the money?
BABY FACE: Probably because he never expected us to escape and go looking for it. Besides, Gentleman Joe liked to think he was smarter than the rest of us. He never figured I could decipher his secret code. *(Reading)* Um-m-m—"Four CS . . . One CM . . . One LB."

CURLY: What does CS stand for?

BABY FACE: Take a look at these walls, Curly. What do you see?

CURLY: Cinder blocks. I get it. C stands for *cinder* or maybe *cement*. But what about S?

BABY FACE: S is for *slabs* or *stones*. If we're right, "Four CS" means *four cement slabs*. Start counting, Curly.

CURLY: But where do we start?

BABY FACE: We'll try everything. *(Consulting paper)* "Four CS"—*four cement slabs*. "One CM" . . . Aha! *One cement moves!* In other words, we count four of these cement blocks, and the next one moves. That must be where he hid the money!

CURLY: What about the next letters—LB? What does LB mean?

BABY FACE: *Lift block*, stupid! Now, start counting. I'll take this side. You take the other.

CURLY: But what if somebody comes? We're unarmed.

BABY FACE: And we're going to stay that way so nobody gets hurt. Besides, who would come poking around an abandoned garage on a vacant lot? *(Voices are heard off.)*

SHIRLEY *(Offstage):* Hurry and open the door! What's the matter? Won't the key work?

CANDY *(Offstage):* Give me time!

BABY FACE: Hey, someone's coming. We have to get out of here.

CURLY: Too late. Get out of sight. *(They crouch behind bench as door opens.)*

CANDY *(Entering):* There, that does it. *(She starts to center, suddenly sees CURLY and BABY FACE, and drops pail she is carrying.)* Help! Help! Robbers! *(SHIRLEY pushes past CANDY, carrying mop and pail.)*

SHIRLEY *(Impatiently):* Oh, good grief! Be quiet, Candy. (JEN, DONNA, *and* KATE *follow* SHIRLEY *into garage, all carrying mops, pails, and boxes.* JEN *holds folder of papers.* SHIRLEY *sees* BABY FACE *and* CURLY *and speaks to them scoffingly.)* Robbers, indeed! You two have a lot of nerve. Maybe you can fool Candy and the others with those masks, but not me. I'd know you anywhere.

CURLY *(Getting up and moving toward door):* Let's beat it! The kid is wise to us. (BABY FACE *stands.)*

SHIRLEY: You bet I am, so don't bother to put on any silly gangster act. I never thought Jerry Mason would stoop to sending his big brother and his buddy to spy on us! No wonder you're wearing masks, you big bullies! You should be ashamed to show your faces!

BABY FACE: Now wait a minute, little girl!

SHIRLEY *(To other girls):* What do you say, girls? Now that we have these two big sophomores with us, let's put them to work.

BABY FACE *(Outraged):* Sophomores!

JEN: Good idea, Shirley. They can help us clean up this place. (JEN *puts folder of papers on the workbench; others put down boxes and push pails and mops toward* BABY FACE *and* CURLY.)

CANDY: They really had me fooled for a minute.

DONNA: I was scared, too, Candy. Why are they wearing masks?

SHIRLEY: Part of the big plan to scare us off! Jerry and his Super-Sleuths are determined to have this old garage for their meeting place, but the FBI got here first.

CURLY *(Alarmed):* The FBI?

KATE: Female Bureau of Investigators!

SHIRLEY *(To* CURLY *and* BABY FACE): As if you didn't

know! Come on. Don't just stand there! *(Pointing)* Stack those boxes along the wall *(Prodding gangsters with mop)*, and hurry up.

JEN: I honestly don't see how you recognized them, Shirley.

SHIRLEY: Elementary, my dear Watson! Elementary!

JEN: Oh, don't be so smart! And stop calling me *Watson!* Just because your name is Shirley Holmes, you don't have to talk like *Sherlock* Holmes. You know my name is Jen.

SHIRLEY: But your last name *is* Watson, and you *are* my first assistant detective.

CURLY *(Aside to* BABY FACE): Detective! What is she talking about?

BABY FACE: Easy, Curly! It's just some game they're playing.

DONNA: Is that so?

CANDY: I'll have you know we're real, honest-to-goodness investigators with half a dozen cases to our credit.

DONNA: And our business is growing. That's why we need this garage for our headquarters.

SHIRLEY: And we're going to have it, too. In spite of Jerry Mason and his Super-Sleuths. *(Offstage howl of sirens is heard and continues.)*

BABY FACE: What's that?

CURLY: Police sirens! Run for your life!

BABY FACE: Pardon our hasty departure, ladies, but we have urgent business elsewhere. (CURLY *and* BABY FACE *dash out and slam door shut.)*

DONNA: Well, what was that all about?

KATE: I don't know, but there goes our extra help.

CANDY: Something tells me, Kate, that we're just as well off without that pair.

JEN: You're right, Candy. Even Shirley can't explain how she recognized them.

SHIRLEY: I have my methods, but if we stand here talking all day, we'll never get this place straightened up. *(Offstage knocking in rhythmic pattern is heard.)*

DONNA: Do you think they've come back?

SHIRLEY: Open the door and see. *(As* DONNA *opens door,* JERRY *steps in waving a white flag on a stick.)*

DONNA: Jerry Mason, you get out of here and stay out.

JERRY: Have a heart, Donna! Look! We come under a flag of truce.

KATE: Do you have the rest of your outfit?

JERRY: Sure thing! Didn't you hear our bicycle sirens? *(Calls off)* Super-Sleuths, advance and report. *(*ALF, LARRY, BRUCE *and* ADAM *enter.)*

ALF: Alf Lyman reporting, sir.

LARRY: Larry Briggs reporting, sir.

BRUCE: Bruce Harmon reporting, sir.

ADAM: Adam Powers reporting, sir.

JERRY: All present and accounted for! Now, what can we do to help?

DONNA: Help?

JERRY: Sure, that's why we came. We thought we could lend a hand.

SHIRLEY: A likely story!

JEN: After that mean trick you just played on us?

ALF: Trick? What trick?

LARRY: We haven't been near this place all day.

CANDY: Oh, don't act so innocent!

SHIRLEY: I suppose you didn't send Jerry's brother and his buddy to scare us away from here.

JERRY: What are you talking about? My brother is away on a basketball trip, and so are most of his friends.

DONNA *(Sarcastically):* Then I guess we only imagined

we saw two high school guys in here with masks over their faces.

BRUCE (*To* JERRY): They must mean those two guys who almost knocked me over just now, in the alley.

JERRY: They were no friends of ours! Honest!

SHIRLEY: But I could have sworn I recognized them. I could see their high school letters on their shirts, showing through their sweaters—SPHS!

CANDY: Maybe they weren't from the high school. Maybe they were robbers after all.

JERRY: Did they take anything?

ALF: Is anything missing?

DONNA: Let's take a look. *(All scatter to look in various places.)*

SHIRLEY: There's so much junk in here, we would hardly know if anything is missing or not.

ALF *(Looking in box):* This is full of pots and pans and groceries.

JEN: That's mine. I was going to make some fudge.

JERRY: I thought this was to be a business office, official headquarters for your silly FBI meetings.

KATE: There's no law against making fudge.

BRUCE: I'm all for it! (JERRY *picks up folder of papers and robbers' direction sheet from workbench.*)

JERRY *(Looking at paper):* What is this? (ALF *looks at paper in* JERRY's *hand.*)

ALF: Um-m. Looks like some sort of code.

JERRY: Right! *(Reading)* "Four CS, One CM, One LB, One CC, Two SQCB."

JEN *(Snatching paper away from him):* Secret code! That's my fudge recipe!

JERRY: Fudge recipe!

JEN: I guess it fell out of my folder.

ALF: I thought it was a cryptogram.

JEN: That's how much you boys know about cooking! CS is cups of sugar, CM is a cup of milk and LB is a lump of butter.

KATE *(Scanning paper):* I guess CC is a cup of cocoa.

DONNA: Two SQCB. That must be two squares of chocolate, but what's the *B*?

CANDY: *B* for *Bitter.* Even I know you always use bitter chocolate for fudge.

BRUCE: All this is making me hungry. Why don't you go ahead and make the fudge while we pitch in on the clean-up job?

JEN: O.K. I only hope this hot plate works. *(Pretends to turn it on)* It seems all right.

CANDY *(Joining her):* Let me help you, Jen. *(Girls start to make fudge.)*

ALF: If this radio is working, we can have some music while we work. *(Fiddles with radio; static is heard.)*

SHIRLEY: I still don't understand this great burst of generosity.

KATE: Neither do I, not when you were so determined to have this place for your Super-Sleuths meetings.

BRUCE: There's an old saying: "When you can't lick 'em, join 'em!"

SHIRLEY: Nothing doing! The FBI is strictly female, and it's going to stay that way.

JERRY: Oh, come on, Shirley, you know the best detectives in the business are men.

DONNA: Is that so? How about the Mystery of the Missing Notebook and the Case of the Kidnapped Kitten? We solved those without any help from you.

JERRY: Kid stuff! Now, we Super-Sleuths—(RADIO ANNOUNCER, *offstage or over mike, breaks in.)*

ANNOUNCER: "We interrupt this program to bring you a special news bulletin."

ALF: This old radio works pretty well.

ANNOUNCER *(Continuing):* "Fairview Police are on the lookout for Baby Face Boyd and Curly Smith, who escaped from the State Prison Hospital Squad early this morning. Officials have reason to believe the two men may be heading for Fairview in an attempt to recover the money from the great payroll holdup last spring. The missing prisoners are described as short, slight, and extremely youthful in appearance. A reward of five thousand dollars is offered for their capture or information leading to their arrest."

CANDY: Shirley, those two were the bandits! I'm sure of it! (ALF *turns off radio.*)

JERRY: Some detectives! You and your Female Bureau of Investigators!

ADAM: FBI! Ha, ha! Flea-Brained Idiots would be more like it!

ALF: You had those two guys right here, and you let them get away.

SHIRLEY: How could I have been so stupid! I thought those letters on their shirts—SPHS—stood for South Penn High School, not State Prison Hospital Squad!

DONNA: But what were they doing in this garage?

ADAM: Looking for the hidden money.

JERRY: Then it must still be here. We have to turn this place inside out! *(They all begin to look around frantically.* JEN *continues stirring fudge.)*

ALF: Hey, Larry, give me a hand with these stepladders and this lumber. *(They move ladders and lumber aside and reveal a cupboard.)*

SHIRLEY *(Astonished):* I never knew that old cupboard was there. (JEN *comes forward carrying pan of fudge.)*

JEN *(Shaking her head):* Look at this mess. Something's wrong with this fudge.

JERRY: Never mind the fudge now—not at a time like this.

JEN: But look at it—I can hardly stir it. I don't understand what happened to it.

CANDY: You must have made a mistake in the recipe. *(She walks over to bench and begins to leaf through papers in folder.)*

JEN: I put in everything that recipe called for.

SHIRLEY: The recipe. Where is it, Jen?

JEN: Right there next to the hot plate. What are you all excited about?

SHIRLEY *(Picking up recipe excitedly and scanning it quickly):* Jen, you've solved the mystery!

JEN: I've done *what*?

SHIRLEY: Your fudge has solved the mystery. Jerry was right. This *is* a secret code. I didn't notice this before.

LARRY: Notice what?

SHIRLEY: The proportions are all wrong for fudge. No wonder the fudge is too thick! Just one cup of milk would never dissolve four cups of sugar! And why would you use cocoa and bitter chocolate in the same recipe?

CANDY *(Excitedly, as she pulls piece of paper from folder and begins waving it around):* Here's your recipe, Jen. It was in your folder. It's labeled "Recipe for Chocolate Fudge."

DONNA: If this paper is really the clue to the hidden money, those men will come back.

KATE: I'm scared! Let's get out of here.

JERRY: You're right, Kate. This is a man's job. You girls go home, and let the Super-Sleuths take over.

SHIRLEY: Not on your life! Kate, you run to the nearest phone and call the police. Donna, you go down to the corner and try to find Officer Higgins. I'll lock the door after you. (DONNA *and* KATE *exit.*)

JERRY: If we can only figure out this crazy code. *(Reading)* "Four CS"—those letters must stand for something right here in this garage.

BRUCE: C! C! What begins with the letter C? Ceiling . . . cement . . . counter . . .

SHIRLEY: Cupboard! *Cupboard* starts with a C! Quick, let's look!

ALF: But it says "Four CS." There's only one cupboard.

SHIRLEY: But maybe it has four shelves.

JERRY: That's it! "Four CS"! Fourth cupboard shelf!

LARRY *(Climbing on packing box):* Let me look!

JEN: Do you see anything?

LARRY: A lot of cobwebs. Wait a minute. There's something shoved back here. *(Takes down a bag, and hands it to* BRUCE) Don't drop it. It's heavy.

BRUCE: It's made of some heavy material.

ADAM: Probably canvas.

SHIRLEY: Of course! It all fits. CM—*canvas mailbag.*

BRUCE *(Opening bag):* It's full of money!

ALL *(Ad lib):* We've found it! The holdup money! It's here! *(Etc.)*

LARRY *(Still groping on shelves):* Here's a big flat book of some kind. *(Hands book to* JEN)

JEN *(As she takes it from him):* It's a ledger book. That must be what LB stands for. *(She opens ledger.)* There's more money between the pages!

BRUCE *(To* LARRY): Anything else up there?

LARRY *(As he gropes in cupboard):* I think so. Yes, here's a can. *(Hands it to* CANDY)

CANDY: It's a coffee can. That's the CC. *(Opens can and*

looks inside) More money!

LARRY *(Making final sweep of shelves with his hand):* Wait a minute. Here are two boxes. *(Takes them down and hands them to ALF. There is a sound of rattling at door.)*

ADAM: Sh-h! Someone's at the door.

CANDY: Maybe the girls are back with the police.

SHIRLEY: No. They would have given us the signal.

CURLY *(Calling from offstage):* Open up in there.

JERRY: You girls take cover. *(There is a loud banging on the door.)*

BABY FACE *(Calling from offstage, angrily):* Open up, and be quick about it!

CANDY *(As banging continues):* They may break down the door.

SHIRLEY *(Seizing canoe paddle from table):* Then let's get ready for them! Jen, you take the baseball bat. Candy, you get that tennis racket.

CURLY *(Calling from offstage):* This is a countdown! Ten seconds, and we're coming in!

BRUCE: They mean business!

JERRY: Quick. Set up those ladders at either side of the door. (ALF *and* ADAM *set up ladders, as* CURLY *begins a slow countdown from offstage.)* I think we're about to make the catch of the season.

ALF: What are you going to do?

JERRY *(Tossing volleyball net to* ALF*)*: You and Adam get up on the ladders, stretch this net across the doorway and drop it over their heads as they come through the door. (ALF *takes net from* JERRY, *hands one end to* ADAM. *They mount ladders and stretch net across doorway.* BRUCE *and* LARRY *each grab a mop, as girls line up at either side with their "weapons.")*

SHIRLEY: We're ready for them now, Jerry.

JERRY *(Looking over group):* All set? *(Pause)* Here we go! (JERRY *opens door, and* BABY FACE *and* CURLY *almost fall through doorway.* ALF *and* ADAM *drop volleyball net over them, and both robbers become entangled in it. The others rush at them, bringing them to floor.)*

BABY FACE *and* CURLY: Help! Help! (JERRY *sits astride* CURLY, *and* BRUCE *sits on* BABY FACE.)

JERRY: Had enough?

CURLY *and* BABY FACE *(Ad lib):* Yes! Let us up! Get off my back! (*Etc.* KATE *enters, followed by* DONNA, OFFICER HIGGINS *and* OFFICER RYAN.)

KATE: I hope we're in time.

HIGGINS: What in the world is all this about?

RYAN: What's going on here, anyway?

DONNA: These are the men I told you about! They're the prisoners you're looking for. (JERRY *and* BRUCE *stand up.* BABY FACE *and* CURLY, *still entangled in net, sit up.*)

HIGGINS: They answer the description all right. *(Takes out handcuffs)*

JERRY *(Pointing to table):* And you'll find the missing money right there, too. (BABY FACE *and* CURLY *untangle net and stand.* HIGGINS *starts to put cuffs on them.*)

BABY FACE: They found the money! How did you break the code?

CURLY: How did you kids know that "Four CS" meant *four cement slabs?*

SHIRLEY: It didn't. It stood for *fourth cupboard shelf,* and that's where we found the money.

BABY FACE *(Looking at cupboard):* That cupboard wasn't even here when we were looking.

RYAN: Now, kids, can you fill us in on all this code

business? I'll have to put it in my report.

DONNA: Well, we surprised these two men here in the garage, but mistook them for high school guys playing a joke on us.

SHIRLEY: They ran off when they heard the sirens and left a piece of paper here with what turned out to be a code that led us to the money.

ALF: I turned on the radio, and we heard the special news bulletin about the escape of these two characters.

JERRY: And Shirley broke the code and led us to the loot . . . with the help of her Female Bureau of Investigators.

SHIRLEY: But it was you and your Super-Sleuths who figured out how to trap Baby Face and Curly in the volleyball net.

HIGGINS: Yes, *that* was a new idea to me. And a great one.

JERRY: Not very new, Officer! Have you ever seen pictures of Roman gladiators trapping their enemies in nets?

HIGGINS: Now that you mention it, I did see something like that in a movie last week. But just the same, you can take credit for making it work here. *(Takes prisoners' arms)*

RYAN *(As he starts to stack money into carton):* And this is the money from the payroll robbery, all right. You kids deserve a lot of credit . . . and the reward.

HIGGINS *(Starting toward door with* CURLY *and* BABY FACE): Come on, Ryan. We have to get this pair down to Headquarters. *(Turning to* JERRY *and* SHIRLEY) And we'll want you all to come down later and tell the whole story to the Chief.

RYAN: And there's a reward, too, you know. *(He picks up*

carton and walks over to prisoners and takes one by the arm.)

ALL *(Ad lib):* Reward! We forgot all about it! Great! *(Etc.)*

HIGGINS: Five thousand dollars—and you kids have certainly earned it.

RYAN: Let's go, Higgins. *(To* BABY FACE *and* CURLY*)* Come on, you two. March! (HIGGINS *and* RYAN *lead prisoners to door.)*

BABY FACE *(As he goes off):* Trapped by a bunch of kids! *(Exits)*

CURLY *(Following):* And they made everything sound so easy! *(Exits)*

HIGGINS *(Turning at door):* I'll send a car for you kids in about twenty minutes. (HIGGINS *and* RYAN *exit.)*

ALF: If we get all that money, the Super-Sleuths can build a super-duper clubhouse!

KATE: And what about the FBI?

SHIRLEY: I've been thinking about the FBI, Kate. Maybe we should make a few changes. It's pretty nice to have some boys around, when you need them.

JERRY: And I've been thinking, too, Shirley. I doubt if the Super-Sleuths could solve a mystery with a pan of fudge.

JEN: Are you talking about a merger?

SHIRLEY: That's what I have in mind. We'll make an unbeatable force.

CANDY: But we'd have to change our name. We could call ourselves the Fairview Bureau of Investigators if we joined with the boys.

JERRY: All in favor?

ALL *(Ad lib):* Yes! Great! Hooray! *(All cheer as curtain closes.)*

THE END

Vicky Gets the Vote

Characters

VICKY DEANE, *campaign chairman*
BOB LIGHTNER, *candidate for Junior Mayor*
JIM, *campaign manager*
EDITH ⎫
CARL ⎪
ARCHY ⎪
GEORGE ⎬ *committee members*
THELMA ⎪
FRANK ⎪
MIMI ⎭
UNCLE JOE, *State Senator*
MR. DEANE
MRS. DEANE

SETTING: *The Deane living room, furnished with couch,
chairs, tables, lamps, etc. Writing table is downstage;
telephone is on small table upstage. Table, center, is
covered with leaflets, campaign buttons, and papers.
Poster tacked on wall reads* LIGHTNER FOR MAYOR.

AT RISE: VICKY *is sitting at table, center.* BOB, JIM,
EDITH, CARL, ARCHY, GEORGE, THELMA, FRANK,
and MIMI *are scattered around the room. They all
wear large campaign buttons.*

147

VICKY: Will the meeting of the Lightner Campaign Committee come to order? I think we have everything under control. The posters are up, and you will distribute the leaflets and buttons tomorrow. Edith, will you please write a letter to Mr. Zinn and thank him for printing them for us?

EDITH: I never knew being secretary for a campaign committee could be so much work.

VICKY: That's because we're really doing this campaign up right.

BOB: I certainly want to thank everyone on this committee for working so hard. If I win, I'll owe it to all of your hard work—especially to Vicky. *(Smiles at her)* We're lucky to have the niece of a state senator as our campaign chairman.

VICKY: I don't know about that, Bob. But I've heard Uncle Joe say that one of the most important things about a campaign is to keep the candidate's name before the public as much as possible.

BOB: And that slogan—"Light the Way with Lightner!"—has to be a winner.

CARL *(Laughing):* You're just lucky to have a name that was so easy to work into a slogan.

THELMA: Polly Douglas did the best she could with her slogan, but it was hard for her to come up with a good one.

ARCHY: "Golly! Golly! Vote for Polly!" *(Shakes his head)* She'll never win with that.

VICKY: It takes more than a slogan to win an election. The most important part of our campaign is tomorrow's rally. That's why I called this special meeting, so we could practice.

GEORGE: We're really going to show that junior high crowd we mean business.

MIMI: They think we're just a bunch of babies!

VICKY: Our plan will fall flat unless we keep it an absolute secret and pull it off as a big surprise. Now, let's run through it just the way we'll do it tomorrow. Mimi, you stand over there by the light switch and turn off the lights on cue. (MIMI *goes to switch.*) Everybody set?

ALL *(Ad lib):* We're set. Ready. Let's go. *(Etc.)*

VICKY: O.K. Jim, as Bob's campaign manager, you'll make the first speech. (JIM *steps forward with sheet of paper.*)

JIM *(Reading to audience):* Mr. Chairman, members of the faculty, and student body: As you all know, this is the first time in the history of Valley View School that the middle grades have participated in a school election. The junior high students have had elections for Mayor, Assistant Mayor, Clerk, Treasurer, and other offices. But now for the first time we're going to vote and elect a Junior Mayor, Junior Assistant Mayor, Junior Clerk, and Junior Treasurer. This is a great step forward in making our school more democratic. We middle graders have made every effort to find the best possible candidates for every office. As campaign manager for the office of Junior Mayor, I am very proud of my candidate. In the six years that he has been a student at Valley View, he's had a great record. Last year he received a merit award as the pupil who had made the greatest progress in his class, and he also received the Junior Citizenship Award. My candidate is an outstanding student, active in sports, and a member of the elementary school orchestra. He is well liked and respected. Do yourself and your school a favor by voting for him. I now present my candidate for Junior Mayor of Valley View—Robert Lightner!

(VICKY *signals to* MIMI. *Lights go out. All turn on
flashlights and wave them in time to the music of
"Tramp, Tramp, Tramp."*)
ALL *(Singing):*
>Light, light, light the way with Lightner!
>Bob's the boy who's here to stay.
>Vote for Lightner and you'll see
>What a great school this will be!
>Vote for Lightner on the big Election Day!

(During the song, MRS. DEANE, MR. DEANE, *and*
UNCLE JOE *enter. All applaud.)*

UNCLE JOE: Very fine! Very fine, indeed!

MR. DEANE: What in the world are you doing here in the
dark? (MIMI *turns on the light switch; lights go up on
stage.*)

MRS. DEANE: I hope we haven't interrupted your meeting.

VICKY: Uncle Joe! *(Runs to him)* What a surprise!

UNCLE JOE *(Smiling and hugging her):* I'm just on my
way to Philadelphia, and thought I'd drop in for a visit
with my favorite niece. That was great singing. What's
it all about?

VICKY: Uncle Joe, you came at just the right time. We're
in the midst of an election.

MR. DEANE: That's all she talks about. She must have
gotten her political ideas from you.

UNCLE JOE: Election for what?

VICKY: The middle grades at Valley View are holding
school elections, and for the first time ever we're vot-
ing for our own junior officers. *(Pointing)* Uncle Joe,
I'd like you to meet our candidate for Junior Mayor,
Bob Lightner. Bob, this is my Uncle Joe, Senator
Ames.

UNCLE JOE: Glad to meet you, Bob.

BOB: Thank you, sir. I've never met a real Senator before.

UNCLE JOE (*Laughing*): Well, I hope I'll be a real Senator after Election Day. I'm in the midst of my re-election campaign right now, you know.

VICKY: We're betting on you, Uncle Joe.

UNCLE JOE: That's one thing about elections, Vicky. You can never be sure until the last vote is counted.

BOB: That's what I keep telling Vicky.

UNCLE JOE: What was all that singing when I came in?

GEORGE: That was our campaign program for the rally tomorrow. Each campaign manager is allowed a two-minute speech, a stunt of some kind, and then the candidate speaks for two minutes.

THELMA: Vicky made up the stunt and the song.

ARCHY: Light the way with Lightner! That's Bob's slogan.

UNCLE JOE: Very good. I'd like to hear your speech, Bob. Maybe I can give you some tips.

BOB: O.K. (*Takes paper and reads*) Mr. Chairman, members of the faculty, and fellow students: You have all seen my posters on the bulletin boards and heard my campaign slogan: "Light the Way with Lightner." But there is one thing I would like to point out to you. In the stunt which you have just seen, one flashlight would not have been very effective. Each light is small and flickering by itself. But all the flashlights, working together, made a good, strong beam. And that's the way it is with this election. I cannot light the way to good school government by myself. It will take all of us, working together, to do that. If I am elected Junior Mayor, I promise I will do everything I can to get the cooperation of all grades and all classes, so that, together, we can light the way to a better, happier Valley View School. *(All applaud.)*

UNCLE JOE *(Clapping* BOB *on the shoulder):* Excellent, Bob! Excellent!

VICKY *(To committee):* Well, gang, it looks as if our rehearsal has been a success. Now, remember, not a word to anyone about this. Keep your flashlights out of sight till the very last minute. One blink at the wrong time would spoil the whole effect.

ALL *(Ad lib):* O.K. We understand. *(Etc.)*

MR. DEANE: Perhaps Uncle Joe has something to say to your committee.

ALL *(Applauding):* Speech! Speech!

UNCLE JOE: Well, boys and girls, Election Day has always been a great day for Americans. In the past, it was a day of torchlight processions, fireworks and parades to celebrate the right to vote in a free election. Right now, you are experiencing the thrill of an election in which you have the right to vote. Some day you will have the same right as American citizens. I hope all of you will learn to appreciate and preserve that right. Election Day is the one day of the year when we are truly equal, when we all have equal power. Every man's vote counts the same. *(All applaud.)*

BOB: That was a fine speech, Senator Ames.

UNCLE JOE: Thank you, Bob.

VICKY: Thanks, Uncle Joe. *(To committee)* And now, if there is no further business, I declare the committee meeting adjourned. (EDITH, CARL, ARCHY, GEORGE, THELMA, FRANK, *and* MIMI *start to exit.)*

ALL *(Ad lib):* Goodbye. See you later. So long. *(Etc.)*

BOB: Thanks, Vicky, for all your help.

JIM: I'm sure our stunt will go off without a hitch.

BOB: It was good to meet you, Senator Ames.

JIM: That goes for me, too, Senator.

UNCLE JOE: The same to you.

BOB: Goodbye, Vicky. See you tomorrow. (BOB *and* JIM *exit.*)

UNCLE JOE: Well, Vicky, I hope your candidate wins.

VICKY: He just can't lose, Uncle Joe.

UNCLE JOE: Don't say that, Vicky. Anything can happen in an election.

VICKY: But he's the best candidate.

UNCLE JOE: It's still up to the voters to elect him.

MRS. DEANE: I've never seen you so enthused about anything as this election, Vicky.

UNCLE JOE *(Sitting):* No American is too young to learn that voting is both a privilege and a responsibility. (MR. DEANE *sits.*)

MRS. DEANE *(Sitting):* How is your campaign shaping up, Joe?

UNCLE JOE: Pretty well. It all depends now on getting out the vote.

VICKY *(Sitting):* What do you mean, Uncle Joe? "Getting out the vote?"

UNCLE JOE: Getting as many people as possible to vote on election day.

VICKY *(Puzzled):* But doesn't everybody vote? That is— everybody who is old enough?

UNCLE JOE *(Smiling):* I only wish they did, Vicky. In the last Presidential election millions of voters didn't even bother to cast their votes.

MR. DEANE: And that was a *Presidential election.* Last year at our local primaries only thirty-three percent of the voters turned out.

VICKY: But why?

UNCLE JOE: Lots of reasons: sickness, lack of interest, no candidate they like. . . .

MRS. DEANE: Some people I know just can't be bothered. They forget . . .

VICKY: But how could you forget about an important thing like voting?

MR. DEANE: You're enthusiastic, Vicky, because this is your first big election. It's the first time you've had the right to vote.

UNCLE JOE: As a matter of fact, I doubt if all the students in your school will vote in your election.

VICKY *(Upset):* But they have to!

MR. DEANE: Oh, no. They don't have to vote. Nobody can make them vote. How they vote, or whether they vote at all is a matter of individual decision.

UNCLE JOE: It's really an issue for all of us to worry about. Of all the countries in the world, the United States has one of the lowest percentages of voters who actually vote.

VICKY: That's terrible!

UNCLE JOE: Maybe when you grow up, you and your friends will take voting more seriously. *(Looks at watch, then jumps up)* It's later than I thought. Here it is—time to leave, and I haven't told you why I really came.

VICKY: What do you mean?

UNCLE JOE: I came to ask to borrow you, Vicky, for next Tuesday afternoon. I would like you to sit on the platform with me at the big rally in Capital City.

VICKY *(Excited):* Oh, Uncle Joe! That would be wonderful! *(Abruptly)* But what about school?

MR. DEANE: I think this trip could come under the heading of an educational experience.

UNCLE JOE: They're going to open the new bridge in Capital City, and I'm allowed to invite the lady of my choice to cut the official silver ribbon when I make the dedication speech.

VICKY (*Hopping up and down*): Oh, Mother! May I go?

MRS. DEANE: It's fine with me. What do you think, Fred?

MR. DEANE (*Smiling*): I think it's quite an honor.

UNCLE JOE: Then it's all settled. I'll pick you up next Tuesday morning at ten. Now I must be on my way. Good luck with your campaign, Vicky. I'll see you Tuesday.

VICKY: I can hardly wait! The election is on Monday, and this is on Tuesday! It's super!

MR. DEANE (*To* UNCLE JOE): I'll see you out to the car.

UNCLE JOE: If you want to get in touch with me in the meantime, I'll be at the Washington Hotel in Capital City.

VICKY: Goodbye, Uncle Joe.

UNCLE JOE: Goodbye. (*All exit but* VICKY. *Phone rings. She answers.*)

VICKY (*Into phone*): Hello. . . . Yes, this is Vicky. . . . Oh, hello, Bob. . . . No, I haven't seen the paper. Ours hasn't come yet. . . . What furnace are you talking about? . . . But they can't do that! They simply can't. (JIM *enters, waving paper.*)

JIM: Vicky, have you seen the paper?

VICKY (*Into phone*): Wait a minute, Bob, Jim just came in. . . . O.K., I'll call later. (*Hangs up*)

JIM: Listen to this: "Pupils of Valley View to Have Extra-Long Weekend. School closed Friday and Monday to install new furnace!"

VICKY: But they can't do that!

JIM *(Puzzled):* Why not? They've been waiting for the new parts for that furnace for weeks. Now we have a day off!

VICKY: But, Jim, that means the election will be postponed from Monday to Tuesday.

JIM: So what? It won't make any difference.

VICKY *(Upset):* But it makes a difference to me. I won't be here Tuesday.

JIM: You won't be here? Why not? Where are you going?

VICKY: I'm going to Capital City with Uncle Joe.

JIM: You'll just have to tell him you can't go. You'll have to be here to vote.

VICKY: But, Jim, I can't. I'm going to sit on the platform with Uncle Joe at the big rally and cut the ribbon at the new bridge dedication. It's very special.

JIM: It's not as special as this election. Your Uncle Joe himself said nothing was more important than voting.

VICKY: But what's one vote more or less? Bob can win the election without my vote.

JIM *(Angrily):* What? You know this is going to be a close election. Polly Douglas will pull a lot of votes, especially in the fourth and fifth grades. You don't want her to win, do you?

VICKY: Of course not, but . . .

JIM: Then stay home and vote. Good grief! You're the campaign chairman. You have to be there.

VICKY: But my work is finished. I've done everything. The posters are out, the flyers are ready to be distributed. I've written all the speeches, the stunt is ready for the rally. There's really nothing else for me to do.

JIM: Nothing except vote! And that's the most important part! (MR. *and* MRS. DEANE *enter.*)

VICKY: I can't help it. I'm not going to let Uncle Joe down.

MRS. DEANE: What's this about letting Uncle Joe down?

VICKY: Oh, Mother, they're postponing our election all on account of an old furnace!

MR. DEANE: A furnace? What furnace?

JIM: It's all in the paper. The parts have come for the school furnace, and they're closing down the school from Friday till Monday in order to install it.

MR. DEANE: It's about time that furnace was repaired.

VICKY: But, Daddy! It means I won't be here to vote. I've got to go to Capital City with Uncle Joe.

MR. DEANE: You don't exactly *have* to go, Vicky. Nobody's making you.

VICKY: You mean you don't want me to go?

MR. DEANE: I mean you must decide for yourself. Uncle Joe gave you an invitation . . . not an order.

MRS. DEANE: Uncle Joe would understand, Vicky. He knows how much this election means to you.

VICKY: But, Mother, I can't give up that trip just to stay home and vote!

JIM: Is this a real election to you, Vicky, or are you just playing games?

VICKY: Of course, it's a real election. Haven't I worked just as hard as anybody to get Bob Lightner elected Junior Mayor?

JIM *(Disgusted):* Sure you worked hard as long as it was what you wanted to do and you were having fun. Now, when you have something better to do—you forget all about your wonderful right to vote in a school election.

MR. DEANE: Whether it's a school election or a community election, Vicky, voting is serious business.

JIM: What will Bob think if you duck out on election day?

VICKY: Bob doesn't need my one little vote.

JIM: Suppose everybody felt that way? Besides, your Uncle Joe said an election's never won till the last vote is counted.

VICKY: It's Uncle Joe I'm thinking of.

JIM: Your Uncle Joe's a great guy. My Dad says he's the best Senator this state ever had. Somehow, I don't think your Uncle Joe would want anybody sitting beside him on that platform who would walk out on his job as a voter.

VICKY *(Thoughtfully):* Maybe you're right, Jim. *(Sitting down at table)* I guess I just didn't think it through. *(Picks up paper and pen and begins to write. There is a short pause.)*

MRS. DEANE: What are you writing, Vicky?

VICKY: Is Capital City spelled with an *al* or *ol*, Daddy?

MR. DEANE: It's *al*, Vicky.

JIM *(Looking over her shoulder):* "Dear Uncle Joe: I'm sorry about the trip to Capital City, but our election has been postponed until Tuesday and you can understand that I MUST be here to cast my vote." *(Patting her on the shoulder)* Good for you, Vicky. You're really the greatest!

MRS. DEANE: I think this will make Uncle Joe prouder than if you cut all the ribbons on all the bridges between here and California.

VICKY *(Happily):* Someone else can cut the ribbon but no one else can cast my vote! *(Curtain)*

THE END

The Little Nut Tree

Characters

HENRY POOLE
MRS. POOLE, *his mother*
MR. CHARLES POOLE, *his father*
MARY ⎫
ANN ⎪
ELIZABETH ⎬ *children*
GEORGE ⎪
JOHN ⎪
EDWARD ⎭
GUIDE
WOMAN ⎫
MAN ⎪
BOY ⎬ *sightseers*
GIRL ⎭
LORD MAYOR
DON CARLOS, *King of Spain's Minister*
PRINCESS JOANNA, *King of Spain's daughter*
TWO HERALDS
TWO LADIES-IN-WAITING

TIME: *Many years ago in England.*
SETTING: *The garden of Henry Poole, where a little nut*

tree "grows" prominently, right of center.

AT RISE: HENRY *is standing on a stool or stepladder polishing large silver nutmeg which hangs from a branch of tree. Bottles of polish and extra cloths are on small bench near base of tree. Six children—*MARY, ANN, ELIZABETH, GEORGE, JOHN *and* EDWARD—*are working nearby. Three are weeding and three are watering from sprinkling cans.*

CHILDREN *(Singing "The Little Nut Tree" as they work):*
> I had a little nut tree;
> Nothing would it bear,
> But a silver nutmeg
> And a golden pear.
> The children in the village
> Came to work with me
> To water it and care for
> My little nut tree.

HENRY: There! *(Comes down from ladder)* I've finished! How does the nutmeg look?

CHILDREN *(Pausing and looking at tree):* Beautiful! Beautiful!

MARY: I never saw it so bright and shining.

HENRY: I used a new silver polish yesterday.

JOHN: What about the golden pear? It looks pretty dull to me.

HENRY: I'll do that next.

ANN *(Shaking bottle of polish):* I'll shake up the polish for you.

HENRY: Thank you, Ann. I could never take care of my little nut tree without the help of all of you.

GEORGE *(Rising):* There's not a single weed left under the nut tree.

ELIZABETH: I think we've given it enough water for today.

HENRY *(Stooping to feel the ground):* That's just right. Not too wet and not too dry.

EDWARD: Let's move your ladder to the other side so you can reach the golden pear. (EDWARD *and* HENRY *move ladder, and* HENRY *mounts it.)*

MARY: I'll put the polish on your rag and hand it up to you. *(Does so)*

ANN: Be careful! Don't fall.

HENRY *(As he polishes the golden pear):* I won't. (MRS. POOLE, *unseen by children, enters with basket.)*

MRS. POOLE *(Angrily):* Henry Henderson Halliburton Poole! What are you doing up there? *(Children jump in surprise.)*

HENRY *(Almost losing his balance):* Mother, you scared the life out of me!

ELIZABETH: He's polishing the golden pear.

MRS. POOLE: Indeed! Henry, come down this minute!

HENRY: Just three more rubs, and I'll be finished. *(Pauses)* I'm coming. *(Comes down ladder)*

MRS. POOLE: What do you mean by spending your time on that worthless tree when there's work to be done?

HENRY: But, Mother, the silver nutmeg had to be polished.

JOHN: And the golden pear was quite dull.

MRS. POOLE: You're all wasting too much time on this silly tree. There's plenty of work for you to do at home.

MARY: We were just leaving.

MRS. POOLE: Then be on your way.

GEORGE: We'll come back tomorrow, Henry, if you need us.

MRS. POOLE: I can tell you right now he won't need you. His father is going to cut that tree down tonight.

CHILDREN *(Ad lib):* Oh, no! No! He mustn't! He can't do that! *(Etc.)*

HENRY: Please, Mother. Don't let him do such a thing.

MRS. POOLE *(Firmly):* And just tell me why not!

HENRY: There's not another tree like this in the whole kingdom . . . maybe not even in the whole world!

MRS. POOLE: What good is it? We can't eat a silver nutmeg and a golden pear! We can't even sell them, because no one can pick them.

HENRY: But that's a good thing. They would have been stolen long ago if anyone could have pulled them loose from the tree.

MRS. POOLE: I can't argue about it now. There's too much work to be done. And as for you, there is wood to be chopped and water to be fetched from the well. Come into the house at once. *(Exits right)*

EDWARD: I guess we'd better go.

MARY: I am sure your father wouldn't cut down the tree, Henry.

HENRY *(Sadly):* I'm afraid he will, Mary. He says it's not good for anything.

ELIZABETH: Every day more and more people come to see it.

HENRY: Yes, I know. But that's what angers Father. They trample all over the garden and step on the vegetables.

MRS. POOLE *(Calling from offstage):* Henry! Henry!

HENRY *(Calling):* I'm coming, Mother.

CHILDREN *(Ad lib):* Goodbye, Henry. We'll see you soon. Try not to worry. *(Etc. They exit left.)*

HENRY *(As he turns to exit):* Poor little nut tree! Nobody loves you as much as I do. *(He exits right.* GUIDE, *wearing cap with word* GUIDE *on it, enters left with a group of sightseers—*WOMAN, MAN, BOY *and* GIRL.*)*

GUIDE: Right this way, folks. Right this way for the only tree of its kind.

WOMAN *(Pointing):* Is this the tree?

GUIDE: This is it. *(Points)* See the silver nutmeg and the golden pear.

BOY: Are they *real* silver and *real* gold?

GUIDE: Oh, yes, yes indeed.

WOMAN: It's a wonder someone doesn't steal them.

GUIDE: That would be impossible. No one has been able to pick them. Some of the strongest men in the village have tried.

BOY: I'll bet I could pick them. May I try?

GUIDE: You may try, but it's no use.

BOY *(Mounting ladder):* I want the silver nutmeg.

GIRL: Get the golden pear for me. I want the golden pear!

WOMAN: Don't fall.

BOY *(Tugging at nutmeg):* It won't come off.

MAN: Maybe if I shake the tree it will help. *(Shakes trunk of tree)*

MR. POOLE *(Entering):* Here! What's going on here? What are you folks doing in my garden?

GUIDE: They wanted to see the little nut tree.

MR. POOLE: You must all leave at once. This is my property.

GUIDE: We are doing no harm.

MR. POOLE *(Angrily):* I will not have strangers trampling around my garden.

MAN: I think the whole thing is a fake, anyway.

BOY: I don't even believe that nutmeg is real silver.

GIRL: And I'll bet that golden pear is only made of brass.

MAN: If I had that growing in my yard, I'd chop it down.

MR. POOLE: That's just what I am going to do as soon as you people leave.

GUIDE: I'm afraid we'll have to leave, folks. (GUIDE *and sightseers exit left.*)

MR. POOLE (Calling off): Henry! Henry! Bring me my axe. (HENRY runs in.)

HENRY (Upset): Father, what are you going to do?

MR. POOLE: I'm going to chop down this tree.

HENRY (Near tears): Father, please don't cut down my little tree.

MR. POOLE: Henry, we are very poor. We need every bit of land to raise food. And besides, I have some very bad news.

HENRY: What is it, Father? (MRS. POOLE enters, carrying axe.)

MRS. POOLE: Here is your axe, Charles. I heard you asking for it. (Hands axe to him)

HENRY: Father says he has bad news.

MRS. POOLE: What is it, Charles?

MR. POOLE: We will soon be at war with Spain. I will have to leave tomorrow for the army.

MRS. POOLE: Oh, this is terrible, terrible! What shall we do without you?

MR. POOLE: Henry is a big boy now. He will have to take my place. That is why I want to cut down this tree today. He must not waste his time with it, and you'll need the room to grow food.

HENRY: Father, I promise to take good care of Mother and do all the work. Only, please, please, let me keep my little nut tree.

MR. POOLE: It's no use, Henry. My mind's made up. I'll do it right now. Stand back. Out of my way! (As MR. POOLE raises axe, JOHN, GEORGE, ANN, ELIZABETH, MARY, and EDWARD run in.)

CHILDREN (Calling; ad lib): Stop! Wait! Please, wait! (Etc.)

JOHN (Grabbing MR. POOLE's arm): Don't do it, Mr. Poole.

GEORGE: Have you heard the news?

ANN: The most wonderful thing has happened.

HENRY: What is it?

ELIZABETH: The King of Spain's daughter is coming here to your house.

MRS. POOLE: I don't believe it.

EDWARD: She heard about Henry's little nut tree, and she is coming to see it.

MR. POOLE: But we are about to go to war with Spain. The King's daughter would never be coming here.

MARY: But she is!

JOHN: We saw her in her golden coach.

MARY: She'll be here any minute.

ANN: The Lord Mayor himself is riding by her side. *(Offstage sound of trumpets is heard.* HERALDS *enter, with trumpets.)*

1ST HERALD: Make way! Make way for the Princess Joanna! Daughter of His Majesty, the King of Spain.

MR. POOLE: She really is coming! (TWO HERALDS *stand at attention, as* LORD MAYOR *enters with* PRINCESS JOANNA, *followed by* TWO LADIES-IN-WAITING *and* DON CARLOS.)

LORD MAYOR *(To* MR. POOLE*):* Are you Charles Poole?

MR. POOLE: I am, Your Honor.

LORD MAYOR: I have the honor of presenting the Royal Princess, Joanna, daughter of His Majesty, the King of Spain.

MRS. POOLE *(Curtsying):* You are most welcome, Your Highness.

DON CARLOS: I am Don Carlos, the King's Minister.

MR. POOLE *(Bowing low):* At your service.

DON CARLOS: The Royal Princess desires to see with her own eyes the remarkable nut tree that bears nothing but a silver nutmeg and a golden pear.

PRINCESS: I cannot believe there is such a tree in all the world. (HENRY *bows, then eagerly steps forward*.)

HENRY: There it is, Your Royal Highness! *(Points to tree)* See—there is the silver nutmeg and there is the golden pear!

PRINCESS: It is really here! How the silver nutmeg shines in the sun! And the golden pear glows like a ball of fire!

1ST LADY-IN-WAITING: It is truly beautiful, Your Highness.

PRINCESS: And well worth coming hundreds of miles to see! Ever since I heard about the tree from a wandering minstrel, I have thought of nothing else. *(Points to* MR. POOLE) Is this gentleman the owner?

MR. POOLE: The tree belongs to my son Henry, Your Highness.

PRINCESS *(To* HENRY; *smiling):* You must love the tree very much, Henry.

HENRY: Oh, I do, Your Highness. Very much.

PRINCESS: Do you love it too much to part with the silver nutmeg and the golden pear? I would pay you a great sum of money.

HENRY: Alas, I would gladly give them to Your Highness, but . . .

PRINCESS: But what, Henry?

HENRY: But no one can pick them.

DON CARLOS *(Pompously):* Nonsense! *(Turns to* PRINCESS) If Your Highness so orders, I will climb up there and pull them down myself.

MR. POOLE: It's no use, sir. What my son says is so.

PRINCESS: The minstrel who told me about your little nut tree also told me something else.

HENRY: What did he tell you?

PRINCESS: He sang this song for me. Listen. *(She sings.)*

There is a little nut tree;
Nothing will it bear,
But a silver nutmeg
And a golden pear.
And no amount of money
This fruit will ever buy,
Until a lady claims them
With a teardrop in her eye!

HENRY: Do you have a teardrop in your eye, Princess?

PRINCESS (Dabbing at her eyes with a handkerchief): I think so, Henry! Would you care to look?

HENRY (Tilting back her head to look in her eye): Yes, yes! It's as bright as silver . . . as bright as my silver nutmeg!

PRINCESS: Then you will try to get the nutmeg and the pear for me?

HENRY: I'll try at once. (Climbs ladder and easily picks nutmeg; hands it to PRINCESS) Here is the silver nutmeg. (Picks pear and hands it to PRINCESS) Here is the golden pear.

PRINCESS (Excitedly): Thank you! Thank you! I know I am the luckiest princess in the world. Don Carlos, bring in the treasure chest so I may pay Henry.

HENRY: Oh, no, Princess. I will not take your money. I give them to you gladly.

PRINCESS: But you must have a reward.

HENRY (Kneeling): Then tell the King, your father, not to make war on our people. Let us live in peace.

PRINCESS: I shall do so. I will tell my father that you and your people are the kindest folk in the world.

MR. POOLE: A thousand thanks, Your Highness. Now I can stay at home with my family.

LORD MAYOR: This is a great day for our people, Princess.

HENRY: And I can keep my little nut tree forever and ever.

GEORGE: But there's nothing on it.

PRINCESS: I will send the finest gardeners from Spain to help you care for the tree. Perhaps it will bear other fruit in years to come.

LORD MAYOR: And even if it doesn't, it is the most famous tree in the world. I will give orders that this garden be made into a public park where people can come to see the tree which saved them from war.

MR. POOLE: But what about our land and home, Your Honor?

LORD MAYOR: You and your family will move into a mansion in the city.

MR. POOLE: Thank you.

LORD MAYOR: And I further decree that this little nut tree shall be celebrated in song and story throughout our land.

HENRY: Perhaps we could make up a song right now. I'll begin it. *(Sings, and others join in, line by line)*
I had a little nut tree, and nothing would it bear,

MRS. POOLE: But a silver nutmeg and a golden pear.

HENRY: The King of Spain's daughter came to visit me,

MR. POOLE: And all for the sake of the little nut tree.

DON CARLOS: Her dress was all of crimson,

LORD MAYOR: Coal black was her hair.

PRINCESS: I asked you for the nutmeg and the golden pear.

HENRY: I said:
"So fair a princess, never did I see,
I'll give to you the fruit of my little nut tree!"

LORD MAYOR: Excellent! Excellent! Now let's all sing that delightful song together.

ALL *(Note: Autoharp accompaniment is especially effective):*
I had a little nut tree, nothing would it bear,
But a silver nutmeg and a golden pear.
The King of Spain's daughter came to visit me,
And all for the sake of my little nut tree.

Her dress was all of crimson, coal black was her hair.
She asked me for the nutmeg and the golden pear.
I said: "So fair a princess never did I see,
I'll give to you the fruit of my little nut tree."
(Curtain)

THE END

The Glass Slippers

Characters

BUCKLE
KNUCKLE ⎫ *Carefree Cobblers*
CHUCKLE ⎭
MOONEY, *the maker of glass slippers*
MOTHER
TWO DAUGHTERS
CINDERELLA
OLD WOMAN, *Cinderella's Fairy Godmother*
PRINCE
TWO HERALDS
EIGHT CUSTOMERS, *extras*

SCENE 1

TIME: *An afternoon, long, long ago.*
SETTING: *The workshop of the Carefree Cobblers. Counter with shoes is at right. Small table at left has a basin of soapsuds and glass slippers. Stool is at right.*
AT RISE: BUCKLE, KNUCKLE, *and* CHUCKLE *are hammering at shoes on workbench.* MOONEY *is at small table, blowing bubbles from a long pipe.* CUSTOMERS

stand behind display counter center. CUSTOMERS *act out motions in verse.*

CUSTOMERS *(Reciting):*

> Wind, wind, wind your thread,
> And wind, wind, wind your thread,
> And pull, and pull,
> And pull it tight.
> Wind, wind, wind your thread,
> And wind, wind, wind, your thread,
> And sew, and sew,
> And sew it right.
> Tap, tap, tap, tap on each heel.
> Carefree Cobblers work with zeal.

(MOTHER *enters with* TWO DAUGHTERS. CUSTOMERS *select slippers during following conversation.*)

MOTHER: Good morning! Are you the Carefree Cobblers?

COBBLERS *(In unison):* Yes, we are!

BUCKLE *(Rising with a bow):* I'm Buckle.

KNUCKLE *(Rising with a bow):* I'm Knuckle!

CHUCKLE *(Rising with a bow):* And I'm Chuckle.

MOTHER: I have heard you do very fine work. I would like to buy some slippers for my daughters.

BUCKLE: What kind of slippers do you want?

1ST DAUGHTER: They must be the very best.

2ND DAUGHTER: We are going to wear them to the Prince's ball.

COBBLERS: We have all kinds of slippers.

BUCKLE:

> We have slippers of silver,
> And slippers of gold,
> And slippers of satin,
> All made to be sold.

KNUCKLE:

> We have slippers of wood,
> And slippers of straw!
> The prettiest slippers
> That ever you saw.

CHUCKLE:

> We have slippers for work
> And slippers for play,
> And you'll be surprised
> At how little you pay.

1ST DAUGHTER: We want dancing slippers.

KNUCKLE *(With sweeping motion):* Please step up to the counter, and see what we have.

MOTHER *(To* DAUGHTERS*)*: You girls look. *(Sitting on stool)* I'll sit here and rest. You choose whatever pleases you. (CHUCKLE *conducts* DAUGHTERS *to counter, where they examine shoes.)* I want my daughters to be the most beautiful girls at the ball.

BUCKLE: Excuse me, ma'am, but don't you have another daughter at home?

MOTHER: Oh, no. I have only two.

KNUCKLE: There's a very sweet girl who walks by the shop. I thought she was also your daughter.

MOTHER: Oh, you must mean Cinderella. Of course, *she* isn't going.

KNUCKLE: Doesn't she want to go?

MOTHER: I never asked her. But she must stay home and look after the house. Besides, she has no party clothes.

1ST DAUGHTER *(Holding up a pair of slippers):* These gold ones will match my dress, Mother.

2ND DAUGHTER: These silver ones are a little small, but I'm going to wear them anyway. They are so pretty.

MOONEY *(Coming forward with glass slipper):* Wouldn't

one of you young ladies like to try on one of *my* slippers?

MOTHER *(Disdainfully):* Who is this fellow?

BUCKLE: This is our brother, Mooney.

KNUCKLE: Mooney, go back to your corner, and don't bother the ladies.

MOONEY: But my slippers are so beautiful. There are no others like them in the whole world.

1ST DAUGHTER *(Examining slipper):* Why, this slipper is made of glass!

MOTHER: Made of glass! How silly!

2ND DAUGHTER: And look how tiny it is. Not even a child could wear it.

MOTHER *(To* CHUCKLE): Indeed, I'm surprised you have such a fellow in your shop.

CHUCKLE: He's our brother, and if it makes him happy to work in glass, we let him.

MOTHER: Come along, girls. I'm glad you found what you wanted. (KNUCKLE *and* BUCKLE *put slippers in boxes and give them to* DAUGHTERS.)

1ST DAUGHTER: Thank you.

2ND DAUGHTER: Good day to you. (MOTHER *and* DAUGHTERS *exit. Other* CUSTOMERS *select slippers from counter.*)

1ST CUSTOMER: I'll take the ones with the ribbon bows.

2ND CUSTOMER: I'll take the ones with the open toes.

3RD CUSTOMER: I'll take these with the high, high heel.

4TH CUSTOMER: I like the way these slippers feel.

5TH CUSTOMER: I like a shoe to be good and stout.

6TH CUSTOMER: I like the shoes that will not wear out.

7TH CUSTOMER: I like leather that is soft and fine.

8TH CUSTOMER: I like buckles that will really shine. *(Cobblers place shoes in bags, and all* CUSTOMERS *exit.)*

MOONEY *(Sadly):* I'm so disappointed. Nobody even looked at my glass slippers. *(Returns glass slipper to worktable)*

BUCKLE: We've told you that nobody wants a slipper made of glass.

CHUCKLE: They would crack and break in no time.

MOONEY: But they are so beautiful. See how they sparkle in the light. (CINDERELLA *enters, carrying a pair of worn-out shoes.*)

CINDERELLA: Good morning!

BUCKLE: Good morning, ma'am, what can we do for you?

CINDERELLA:
Cobbler, Cobbler, mend my shoe,
Can you make it good as new?
Stitch and sew, mend the toe,
So that I may dancing go!
(Hands shoes to KNUCKLE, *who shows them to others.)*

COBBLERS *(Pantomiming and singing):*
With our hammers, tap, tap, tap.
With our fingers, rap, rap, rap.
(CHUCKLE *hands shoe back to* CINDERELLA.)
Here's your shoe good as new,
And the best of luck to you.

CINDERELLA: Oh, thank you! How much is that?

COBBLERS: Not one cent. We are happy to do it for you.

MOONEY *(Walking to her):* You are Cinderella, aren't you?

CINDERELLA: Why, y-yes, but how did you know?

MOONEY: I've often seen you walk by the shop.

BUCKLE: Your sisters were just in here.

CHUCKLE: Don't you want to go to the ball, too, Cinderella?

CINDERELLA *(Sighing):* More than anything else in the world. But I have to stay at home.

MOONEY: Then why did you want your shoes fixed? They're not for everyday wear.

CINDERELLA: I can't wear them the way they are. And *(Pauses)* if my stepmother should change her mind at the last minute and let me go, I want to be ready.

MOONEY *(Timidly):* Would you like to see my glass slippers, Cinderella? *(Takes her to table and picks up slippers)*

CINDERELLA: Oh, how lovely! They must be the most beautiful slippers in the world.

MOONEY: I think they would fit you. You have such tiny feet. Would you like to try them on?

CINDERELLA: I'd love to, but I don't have time. I must be home before the others finish their shopping. Good-bye, and thank you for mending these old shoes. (CINDERELLA *exits.*)

MOONEY: What a shame Cinderella can't go to the ball!

BUCKLE: She would be the prettiest girl there.

KNUCKLE: And the nicest!

CHUCKLE: And the sweetest!

MOONEY: And she could wear my beautiful glass slippers! (OLD WOMAN *enters.*)

OLD WOMAN *(Stamping her cane on floor):* Service! Service! How about a little service?

ALL: What can we do for you, ma'am?

OLD WOMAN: What do cobblers usually do? Show me some shoes.

BUCKLE: What kind of shoes would you like, ma'am?

KNUCKLE *(Holding up bedroom slippers):* These are very comfortable, ma'am. My grandmother wears this kind all the time.

OLD WOMAN *(Indignantly):* Your grandmother indeed! I want a pair of dancing slippers.

KNUCKLE *(Picking up satin slippers):* These satin ones are very pretty, and they have good sensible heels.

OLD WOMAN: I don't want good sensible heels.

KNUCKLE *(Holding up another pair):* How about this pair? They have nice, broad toes.

OLD WOMAN *(Banging her cane on floor):* I don't want nice, broad toes. I want the prettiest pair of dancing slippers you have in your shop. Don't you have anything in silver or gold?

BUCKLE *(Nervously):* We just sold our last pair of gold slippers, ma'am.

KNUCKLE: And our last pair of silver.

CHUCKLE: We sold them to some young ladies who are going to the Prince's ball.

MOONEY: Are you going to the ball, ma'am?

OLD WOMAN: Don't be ridiculous. I want these slippers for a lonely, unhappy little girl who thinks she isn't going to the ball.

MOONEY: You must mean Cinderella.

OLD WOMAN *(Surprised):* Yes, that is her name.

KNUCKLE: Who are you, ma'am?

OLD WOMAN: I am Cinderella's Fairy Godmother, and she's going to that ball, if it takes my last drop of magic to send her.

ALL *(Jumping up and down and clapping hands):* Hurray! Hurray! Hurray!

OLD WOMAN: Stop that dancing up and down and show me the finest slippers in your shop. There's no time to spare.

MOONEY *(Taking her by the hand):* Please, good, kind Fairy Godmother, please look at *my* slippers. I know they are just what Cinderella wants.

OLD WOMAN (*Looking at glass slippers*): Why, these slippers are made of glass. Not even I have heard of such a thing.

MOONEY: I have worked on them for many years. I know she likes them. She was just in here a few minutes ago.

BUCKLE: She said they were the most beautiful slippers in the world.

KNUCKLE: She said she'd give anything to wear them.

CHUCKLE: Her sisters have such big feet they could never get into them.

OLD WOMAN: That settles it. I'll take them! (MOONEY *wraps slippers and gives them to her.*)

MOONEY: How I should like to see Cinderella dancing in my glass slippers!

BUCKLE: Yes, if only we could see our little friend at the ball.

OLD WOMAN: Meet me in the palace gardens at half-past eight, and I'll change you into fireflies. Then you can fly right up to the palace windows and see everything.

MOONEY: That will be wonderful!

KNUCKLE (*Nervously*): You won't forget to change us back again?

OLD WOMAN: Of course not. What kind of Fairy Godmother do you think I am, anyway?

CHUCKLE: We'll be there at half-past eight.

OLD WOMAN: I'll see you at the palace gate! (*Exits, as curtain falls*)

* * * * *

SCENE 2

TIME: *The next morning.*
SETTING: *Same as Scene 1.*

AT RISE: *Cobblers and* MOONEY *are asleep at their worktables. There is a loud banging offstage.*

CINDERELLA *(Offstage):* Let me in! Let me in!

BUCKLE *(Yawning and stretching):* Ho-hum! What time is it?

KNUCKLE: It must be the middle of the night!

CHUCKLE: Someone is pounding at the door.

CINDERELLA *(Offstage):* Please, please, let me in!

MOONEY *(Jumping up and running to door):* It's Cinderella. (CINDERELLA *enters, carrying one glass slipper.*)

CINDERELLA: Oh, please, please, help me! The most terrible thing has happened.

ALL *(Jumping up; ad lib):* What is it? What happened? *(Etc.)*

BUCKLE: Tell us what happened.

CINDERELLA *(Agitated):* My Fairy Godmother told me to leave the ball by the stroke of midnight, but I was late . . . and . . . oh, dear, I was having such a wonderful time, I forgot to look at the clock. And . . . I . . . I lost one of my beautiful glass slippers. Please, please, Mr. Mooney, can you make me another?

MOONEY: Make you another glass slipper?

CINDERELLA: Yes, please! My beautiful glass slippers are all that I have to remember my wonderful night at the ball.

MOONEY *(Upset):* But it took years for me to make those slippers.

CINDERELLA: But couldn't you hurry, please? *(There is pounding at door.)*

MOTHER *(Offstage):* Let me in! Open this door!

CINDERELLA: Oh, no! That's my stepmother. Quick, I must hide. I don't want her to find me here. *(Crouches behind display table.* KNUCKLE *throws large cloth over her.)*

MOTHER *(Pounding on door):* Let me in! Let me in at once! *(*BUCKLE *opens door, and* MOTHER *and* DAUGH-TERS *rush in.* MOTHER *darts to* MOONEY'S *table.)* Where are those glass slippers that were here yesterday?

1ST DAUGHTER: We must buy them at once.

2ND DAUGHTER: Where are they?

COBBLERS: They have been sold.

MOTHER: Sold! Impossible. Who would wear such things?

MOONEY: Yesterday you made fun of them. Why do you want them now?

1ST DAUGHTER: Last night the Prince found a little glass slipper. He has announced that he will marry the girl who can fit into it.

2ND DAUGHTER: But she must have the mate of the slipper he found.

MOTHER: So if we can buy yours, each of my daughters will have a slipper.

1ST DAUGHTER: I will take the right.

2ND DAUGHTER: And I will take the left.

MOTHER: One of them will have to match up with the one the Prince has. *(Trumpets sound offstage.)*

HERALDS *(Offstage):* Open this door! Open this door in the name of the Prince! *(*BUCKLE *runs to open door, and* PRINCE *enters, carrying glass slipper. He is attended by* HERALDS.*)*

COBBLERS: Your Highness. *(All bow.)*

MOTHER *and* DAUGHTERS *(Curtsying):* Your Highness!

PRINCE *(Holding up glass slipper):* Did one of you cobblers make this glass slipper?

MOONEY: I did, sir. I made the slipper.

PRINCE: I command you to tell me at once who bought it.

MOONEY: An old lady bought them, Your Highness. A very, very old lady.

PRINCE: I don't believe it.

KNUCKLE: He speaks the truth, Your Highness.

PRINCE: I have vowed to marry the young woman who can wear this slipper, but she must be able to show me the mate to it.

MOTHER: Please, Sire. I am sure the slipper belongs to one of my daughters. Will you let them try it on?

PRINCE: Very well. *(Hands slipper to* 1ST HERALD. *He tries to put it on* 1ST DAUGHTER's *foot.)*

1ST HERALD: She can't even get her big toe into it, Your Highness.

2ND DAUGHTER: Oh, please! Let me try!

2ND HERALD *(Taking slipper and trying it on* 2ND DAUGHTER*):* It's no use, Your Highness.

MOTHER: I'm sure if you tried a little harder . . .

PRINCE *(To* BUCKLE*)):* I thought if the slippers were made here, you could lead me to their owner.

BUCKLE: I'm sure we can, Your Highness.

PRINCE: But you told me an old woman bought them.

KNUCKLE: So she did. But *she* did not wear them to the ball last night.

CHUCKLE: The young lady who wore them is right here in our shop. *(Calls)* Cinderella! Cinderella! (CINDERELLA *emerges from her hiding place.)*

MOTHER *and* DAUGHTERS *(In astonishment):* Cinderella!

PRINCE *(Dropping to knees):* My princess! Quick, the slipper! *(Takes slipper from* HERALD *and puts it on* CINDERELLA)

ALL: It fits! It fits!

CINDERELLA (*Excitedly*): And here, my Prince, is the other slipper.

PRINCE (*Rising and taking her by the hand*): On this very day, the lovely Cinderella shall be my bride!

ALL (*Ad lib, except* MOTHER AND DAUGHTERS): Long live Cinderella! Happiness to the Prince and his bride! (*Etc.*)

MOTHER: Come, girls. We will leave at once! (MOTHER *and* DAUGHTERS *exit.*)

CINDERELLA: Please, dear Prince, may I ask a favor?

PRINCE: Anything your heart desires.

CINDERELLA: I ask only that these kindhearted cobblers become the royal shoemakers at the palace.

PRINCE: It shall be done. From now on, they will make all of the shoes for the court and our royal family.

MOONEY: But I can't make anything but glass slippers, Your Highness.

PRINCE: Then you shall be Cinderella's very own shoemaker. From this day forth, she will wear only glass slippers made by your hands.

COBBLERS: This calls for a song! (*They sing to the tune of* "*Fiddle-Dee-Dee.*")

Fiddle-dee-dee, fiddle-dee-dee,
We're all as happy as we can be.
Says the Prince, says he, "Will you marry me,
And live with me contentedly?"
Fiddle-dee-dee, fiddle-dee-dee,
We're all as happy as we can be! (*Curtain*)

THE END

The Miraculous Tea Party

Characters

MINTY
MOTHER
NANCY WEST
BETTY ROSS
RUTH HILL
JANET SIMMS
BILLY EVANS
THE SLEEPING BEAUTY
WALTER, THE LAZY MOUSE
PINOCCHIO
DICK WHITTINGTON
BARTHOLOMEW CUBBINS
MARY POPPINS

SETTING: *Front lawn of the Stevens home. Large umbrella table is right center, and six or seven small chairs are near it. Picket fence is down left. Exit right leads to house.*

AT RISE: MOTHER *is sitting at table, knitting.* MINTY, *dressed up in her mother's hat, fur piece, and high-heeled shoes, wheels doll carriage across stage. Her own shoes stand under table.*

MINTY *(To doll):* Suzabelle, you were a good baby! You never cried once while I was in the store. *(Abruptly)* We'll have to go back again. I've forgotten the eggs. *(Reverses doll cart)*

MOTHER *(Looking up):* I guess you'll just have to go back to the supermarket.

MINTY: It's too late! And anyhow I'm tired of playing grownup. *(Sits at table and takes off shoes)* Besides, my feet hurt! *(Puts on own shoes; takes off hat and fur piece)*

MOTHER: Why don't you cut some paper dolls?

MINTY: I'm tired of paper dolls.

MOTHER: You could draw with your new markers.

MINTY: I'm tired of drawing.

MOTHER: You seem to be tired of everything.

MINTY: I'm tired of playing by myself. Why don't I have anyone to play with?

MOTHER: Because we just moved to this neighborhood, and we don't know any people yet. But don't worry. You'll make friends.

MINTY: How?

MOTHER: I'm sure there are some nice children in this neighborhood. When you see some of them, ask them to come in and play with you. *(Phone rings offstage.)* There's the phone. I must answer it. *(Sets knitting down and exits. MINTY walks left to edge of stage and looks up and down.)*

MINTY: I wish some children would come along right now so I could ask them to play with me. *(Closes her eyes and clenches her fists)* I wish a wish, I make a bow *(Bows)*, I wish somebody would come right now. *(As MINTY opens her eyes, BILLY EVANS enters right, whistling. He carries a ball and glove.)* Here comes a boy! Maybe he'll come in and play with me. *(To BILLY)*

Hello, I'm Minty Stevens. What's your name?

BILLY: Billy Evans. I've never seen you before.

MINTY: That's because we just moved here. Would you like to come in and play with me?

BILLY (*Shaking head*): Sorry, but I have to play ball.

MINTY: I have a ball. I'll play with you.

BILLY: I mean real ball—the kind boys play. I have to be going. So long. (*Exits left*)

MINTY (*Sadly*): And he seemed so nice. (NANCY *enters from left, with jump rope.*) Here comes a girl. (NANCY *stops in front of* MINTY.) Hello! I'm Minty Stevens. We just moved here. What's your name?

NANCY: I'm Nancy West.

MINTY: Would you like to come in and play with me, Nancy?

NANCY: I'd like to, but I have to go to the store for my mother. See you later. (*Exits*)

MINTY: She could have asked me to go along! (*Shakes her head*) I'll have to try again. (RUTH, JANET, *and* BETTY *enter, laughing and talking.*) Hello, girls. I'm Minty Stevens.

RUTH (*Pointing*): This is Betty Ross and Janet Simms, and I'm Ruth Hill. I live across the street from you.

MINTY: I hope we can be friends.

JANET: Sure we can. We might even be in the same grade at school.

BETTY: I hope you're in our room. Miss Gray is the teacher and she's very nice.

MINTY: Would you like to play tag in my yard?

RUTH: We can't now. We're going to Janet's house to watch TV. (*Girls exit.*)

MINTY (*Kicking a stone; angrily*): I hate the boys and girls in this town. I just hate them! They'll never be my friends. I'm going to ask my parents to move away from this horrible place. (MOTHER *enters, with armload of books.* MINTY *runs to her.*) Oh, Mother, let's go back where we came from. Nobody will play with me.

MOTHER *(Putting books on table):* Now, Minty. Don't take it so hard. You might be lonely for a little while, but it won't be long before you meet some of the children and make friends with them.

MINTY: But I met a whole lot, and not one would come in and play with me. Everyone had something else to do or some place to go.

MOTHER: I'm sure they didn't mean to be unfriendly. As soon as you get to know them at school, you'll find you have a lot of things in common. And in the meantime, you're forgetting some of your old friends.

MINTY: All my old friends are back in Park City.

MOTHER: I don't mean those friends. I mean some other old friends you've been neglecting lately.

MINTY: Who?

MOTHER *(Reaching for a book):* Well, here's *The Sleeping Beauty.* You haven't spent any time with her lately. And here's another friend of yours, *Dick Whittington.* (MINTY *picks up books and flips through them.*)

MINTY: Yes, I remember. And you even brought *Pinocchio* and *Mary Poppins!* And *Walter, the Lazy Mouse!* Mother, you've brought all my favorites!

MOTHER: Then why don't you have a tea party for them?

MINTY: How could we have a tea party? After all, they're just books!

MOTHER: Don't say that! They might hear you. I'm going to get some lemonade and cookies while you set the table.

MINTY: Do you mean I should really seat the books as if they were guests?

MOTHER: Why not? You might find them the liveliest guests you've ever had. I won't be long. *(Exits)*

MINTY: It's worth a try. If books are my only friends, I might as well entertain them. *(Arranges books around table)* Now let me see, I'll put Pinocchio here, and Mary Poppins next. Mary's such a great talker, she'll keep Pinocchio entertained. Then next to Mary, I'll put Bartholomew Cubbins! Next comes the Sleeping Beauty. Maybe she'll feel funny coming without the Prince, but there just isn't room. Where can I put Walter? Maybe no one will want to sit next to a mouse. And if Dick Whittington brings his cat, what would happen? *(Sighs)* Well, I'll just have to take the chance. *(Arranges chairs around table)* I'll put Dick Whittington next to the Sleeping Beauty and Walter next to Dick. I'll sit between Walter and Pinocchio.

MOTHER *(Calling from offstage):* Minty, the refreshments are ready.

MINTY: All right, Mother. I'm coming. (MINTY *exits. Almost immediately,* SLEEPING BEAUTY *and* DICK WHITTINGTON *enter.)*

SLEEPING BEAUTY *(Yawning):* Oh, dear! I'm so sleepy. I can hardly keep my eyes open, but this must be the place. Where do we sit?

DICK: We can find our places where the books are set. *(Indicates books on table)* You sit right here, and I am beside you.

SLEEPING BEAUTY: That's fine. *(They sit.)*

DICK: She's invited Walter, the Lazy Mouse, too. He's a very nice mouse but so dreadfully lazy.

SLEEPING BEAUTY: I hope he's not too lazy to come to the party. (WALTER *enters.)*

WALTER: I'm not as lazy as you think, Mr. Dick Whittington. I hope you didn't bring that dreadful cat of yours!

DICK: No danger, Walter. You're perfectly safe. Sit down. Do you know Sleeping Beauty?

WALTER (*Bowing to* SLEEPING BEAUTY): I've never had the pleasure. Charmed, I'm sure. *(Sits)* Don't be nervous. I'll try not to frighten you.

SLEEPING BEAUTY: Thank you. You're very kind.

WALTER: Actually, it's because I'm so lazy. It takes a lot of effort to frighten people, so I don't even try.

DICK *(Looking off):* Here comes Bartholomew Cubbins and Pinocchio. Hello, you two!

BARTHOLOMEW: Good afternoon, friends. *(Takes off hat, puts it on table; he does this several times. There are other hats underneath.)* You'll have to excuse my hats at the table. They just keep reappearing, you know. Is this my place?

SLEEPING BEAUTY: Right here beside me, Mr. Cubbins. *(Points)* Pinocchio, you're over there.

PINOCCHIO: There are two empty chairs. I wonder who else is expected? (MARY POPPINS *enters.*)

MARY POPPINS: Here I am! I'm late, but you know I can never blow in without the East Wind.

PINOCCHIO: Sit near me, Mary, and tell me how you came this time.

SLEEPING BEAUTY: Did you blow in on the tail of a kite?

DICK: Or did you come on a rocket?

MARY POPPINS: Now—no questions. You know I never explain anything.

PINOCCHIO: That's right. She doesn't. Where's our hostess?

WALTER: I think she went inside for the refreshments. I hope she remembers to bring a bite of cheese for me.

(MINTY *enters with a tray of refreshments.*)

MINTY: Oh, I'm so glad to see all of you! How nice that every single one of you managed to come.

BARTHOLOMEW *(Doffing his hat, under which there is another)*: My dear Minty, we wouldn't have missed it.

PINOCCHIO: It isn't every day a puppet gets invited to a party.

DICK *(Pompously)*: As Lord Mayor of London, I had to cancel several meetings, but here I am.

SLEEPING BEAUTY: I couldn't miss talking over old times with my friend, Minty.

MINTY: And you, dear Walter, I'm so glad to see you.

WALTER: I am never too lazy to visit a friend.

MINTY: It's so good to hear that word *friend*. Since we've moved to this town, I don't seem to have any friends at all . . . that is none except you loyal book friends.

BARTHOLOMEW: No friends here? *(Sighs)* That's very sad!

DICK: As Lord Mayor of London, I could pass a law requiring that children of this town make friends with you immediately.

SLEEPING BEAUTY: I could ask my Fairy Godmother to cast a spell on these children.

MARY POPPINS: Maybe I can take things in hand here.

MINTY: Oh, could you, Mary? You always straightened out the Banks family, when they were in trouble.

MARY POPPINS: Quiet! Let me think. *(All are silent while* MARY *thinks.* MINTY *passes lemonade and cookies. During this silence,* BILLY EVANS *enters, tossing his ball into his glove. He stops and stares at tea party.)*

BILLY *(Amazed)*: Will you look at that?

NANCY *(Entering with bag of groceries)*: What's going on, Billy?

BILLY: Look at all those strange people. Who do you suppose they are? (RUTH, BETTY, *and* JANET *enter.*)

NANCY: I haven't the faintest idea. *(To girls)* Did you ever see anything like that?

RUTH: It looks like a tea party.

BETTY: But who are the guests?

JANET (*Pointing to* WALTER): That one looks like a mouse! Is the circus in town?

BILLY: It's that new girl. She's having a party.

RUTH: Just a little while ago she didn't know anybody! (MARY POPPINS *pounds her fist on the table and springs to her feet.*)

MARY POPPINS: I've got it! I've got it! We'll have a thunderstorm.

ALL: A thunderstorm!

MARY POPPINS: Yes, and my friends and I will vanish with the third clap of thunder. Are you ready?

MINTY: You're not going to leave me, Mary, are you?

MARY POPPINS: Not really, Minty. You know your book friends are always as close as your library shelf. Just wait and see. *(Rumble of thunder is heard.)*

NANCY: Listen, it's starting to thunder.

BETTY: There's going to be a storm. *(At second clap of thunder, book characters rise.)*

JANET: I don't want to get wet. *(Points to umbrella table)* Maybe we could run for shelter under that lawn umbrella. *(At third clap of thunder, lights blink out for a second, during which time book characters exit.)*

BILLY: Come on, let's make a run for it. *(Children outside fence run into* MINTY's *yard.)*

JANET: Excuse us for bursting in like this, but we thought we might find shelter under your umbrella.

MINTY: You're welcome, but look—the sky seems to be clearing.

NANCY (*Looking around*): Where did all your guests go? They were here just a minute ago.

MINTY: I guess they had to leave in a hurry.

RUTH: I thought you didn't know anyone in town.

MINTY: I don't. They were my friends, my book friends. I'm sure you must know some of them. (*Picks up book*) There was the Sleeping Beauty. Remember her from your fairy tale books?

NANCY: Oh, yes! (*Takes book from* MINTY, *leafs through it*) I always loved her. This is a beautiful book. It has lots of other stories I've never read.

MINTY: You may borrow it if you like.

NANCY: Oh, could I?

MINTY: Why not? Mother says the nicest part about owning books is sharing them with your friends.

NANCY: Thank you. Maybe you'd like to come over to my house and borrow some of mine?

MINTY: I'd love to.

BILLY: Who was the character who kept his hat on at the table?

MINTY (*Laughing*): That was Bartholomew Cubbins, and you mustn't blame him for keeping his hat on. Every time he takes one off, another pops on in its place.

BILLY (*Laughing*): I'd like to read that story. It sound great.

MINTY: Here. (*Picks up book and hands it to* BILLY) Take it. You'll love it.

RUTH: Give it to me next, will you, Billy? That is—if it's all right with Minty.

MINTY: Of course.

BETTY: Who was that man who sat right here? (*Points to* DICK WHITTINGTON's *chair*)

MINTY: That was Dick Whittington.

BETTY: Didn't he have a cat or something?

MINTY: Yes. I'm glad he didn't bring him to the party. Poor Walter would have been scared to death.

RUTH: Who's Walter?

MINTY *(Picking up book):* This is *Walter, the Lazy Mouse,* by Marjorie Flack—one of my favorites. Would you like to read it?

RUTH: Well . . . if you're sure he'll stay in the book and not go running around.

MINTY *(Amused):* You don't need to worry about Walter. He's too lazy to come out of the book covers.

JANET: But he was here this afternoon. I saw him.

MINTY: That was different. He made a special effort because he knew I needed him. You see, book friends always come when you need them.

BETTY *(Picking up a book):* Why, here's an old favorite of mine—*Pinocchio.*

MINTY: Isn't he wonderful?

BETTY: Funny, and sad, too.

BILLY: I remember when you took up a whole class period in school, telling about *Mary Poppins.*

MINTY: Oh, do you like *Mary Poppins,* too?

BETTY: I love her. Ask you mother if you can come over to my house, and I'll lend you my copies of *Mary Poppins Comes Back* and *Mary Poppins Opens the Door.*

MINTY *(Happily):* I'd love to. But now why don't we sit down at the table and finish the tea party—I mean, the lemonade party?

BILLY: That would be great.

MINTY: Sit where you like, and make yourselves comfortable. *(All sit.)* Here comes Mother with a new batch of cookies.

MOTHER: Why, Minty, I'm so glad to see all your new

friends. *(To others)* I'm sure you and Minty will have a lot in common. *(Sets plate of cookies on table)*

MINTY: We do already, Mother. We have the same book friends. *(Roll of thunder is heard offstage.)*

MOTHER *(Looking up):* Don't tell me we're going to have another storm.

MINTY: That's not a storm, Mother! That's just Mary Poppins giving me the signal that everything is all right and that she and the rest of my book friends will always be ready when I need them! *(Curtain)*

THE END

Production Notes

CIRCUS DAZE
(Play on pages 3–16.)

Characters: 12 male; 3 female.
Playing Time: 25 minutes.
Costumes: Children wear every-day dress. Mr. Darnum and Mr. Cummings wear business suits. Clancy wears an old-fashioned police officer's uniform, false nose and moustache, and carries rubber billy club. Others wear appropriate costumes. Leon and Hugo have torn jackets, and Hugo's face is smudged with soot. Sancho's long cape conceals sword (cardboard); he carries sword handle (cardboard).
Properties: Cardboard barbells labeled 2,000 lbs.; paper; pencil; plates; baton; sword handle; sword; sheet of cardboard with outline of girl drawn on it; stuffed snake; covered reed basket; passes; camera.
Setting: Mr. Darnum's office. Several folding chairs and a table with circus props are at one side. Barbells labeled 2,000 lbs. are on floor. A center are desk and chair. Brightly colored circus posters may complete the setting. Exits are right and left.
Lighting: No special effects.
Sound: Offstage circus music, as indicated in text.

BANDIT BEN RIDES AGAIN
(Play on pages 17–28.)

Characters: 12 male; 8 female.
Playing Time: 20 minutes.

Costumes: Sheriff, Miranda, Cowboys, and Indians wear traditional costumes. Bandit Ben has on dark outfit with black kerchief as a mask. Tilly, Milly, and Willy wear city clothes.
Properties: Sheriff's badge; fishing rod; bait can; workbasket with knitting; camping equipment; bows and arrows; paint cans; peanut butter sandwich; broomstick horses; bag of loot; toy pistol; rope; card.
Setting: Sheriff's office near the Bar-B.Q. Ranch. Crudely-lettered sign at left reads BAR-B.Q. RANCH. Another sign at right reads SHERIFF'S OFFICE. There is a rail fence left, and right, a desk with swivel chair. Large hand bell is on desk.
Lighting: No special effects.

SO LONG AT THE FAIR
(Play on pages 29–38.)

Characters: 3 male, 5 female; 10 or more male or female for Police Officer, Barkers, Attendant, and Children.
Playing Time: 20 minutes.
Costumes: Children and Mrs. Webster may wear everyday clothes. Police Officer wears blue uniform; Carousel Attendant wears dark suit and visored cap, and has badge on jacket; Gypsy wears brightly colored skirt, peasant blouse, and a kerchief on her head. Barkers wear colorful clothes. Johnny wears blue jeans and a red sweater.

Properties: Balloons; pocket notebook; pencil; tickets; small girl's straw hat; bunch of blue ribbons; coin; silver chain with charm attached to it; stuffed animals; paper novelties.

Setting: Scene 1: Bus stop. Sign right reads BUS STOP. There are two benches at rear. Scene 2: Fairgrounds. Four tables representing booths are decorated gaily with crepepaper streamers and colored pennants.

Lighting: No special effects.

Special Note: For the children's carousel, the players form a double circle. Children in the outer circle place their hands on the shoulders of their partners who stand in front of them forming the inner circle. Players in the inner circle join hands. Players in both circles step to the left as the music plays. The music may be sung by the children as they go around in the circle, or may be played on a record. The tempo of the music increases so that the children keep the "merry-go-round" moving as rapidly as possible without dropping their hands.

SOURDOUGH SALLY
(Play on pages 39–50.)

Characters: 7 male; 6 female.

Playing Time: 20 minutes.

Costumes: Modern everyday dress. The boys all wear jeans, and the prospectors wear beards of different colors. Sally wears a coat at the end.

Properties: Five spades, pie pan, letter in envelope.

Setting: The Crane living room in Alaska. One door leads outside, another leads to the rest of the house. A large easel is located at center with a painting of the Alaskan flag. Phone and phone book are on small table.

Lighting: No special effects.

Sound: Doorbell.

THE PAPER BAG MYSTERY
(Play on pages 51-63.)

Characters: 5 male; 8 female.

Playing Time: 20 minutes.

Costumes: Girls wear Girl Scout uniforms; Miss Enders has leader's uniform. Benny and Joe wear jeans, change into coveralls. Officers wear police uniforms.

Properties: 7 large paper lunch bags (there should be a banana and ham sandwich in one); 1 large paper bag (same size as others) filled with fancy necklaces, rings, bracelets, and pins; 2 pairs of coveralls; dust mop; dustpan; carton containing pack of paper bags, box of Life Savers, ballpoint pens, nail polish, pocket-size Kleenex, stickers, beads, bracelets, pins, ball of string, and scissors; bags and packages for Miss Enders; long-handled mop; dust mop and pan.

Setting: Office in deserted school building. At left is a safe with a combination lock. Three desks, chairs, a table, typewriter, and telephone complete the set. Doors are at left and right.

Sound: Banging and pounding.

THE TRIAL OF MOTHER GOOSE
(Play on pages 64–77.)

Characters: 11 male; 8 female; 12 male or female for Children.

Playing Time: 20 minutes.

Costumes: King Cole and Queen wear royal robes and crowns. King has papers in his pocket, and Queen carries a large handkerchief. Mother Goose wears long skirt, apron, shawl, spectacles and cap. The Mother Goose characters wear appropriate costumes. Fiddlers are dressed alike; each carries a violin. Soldiers and Herald wear uniforms. Prince George wears peasant costume and big hat; carries crown in his pocket. Cook and Mary wear aprons. Children may wear everyday clothes.

Properties: Silver bowl; wooden pipe; saucepan; 3 violins; scroll; pen.

Setting: Kitchen of King Cole's palace. Up right is a fireplace with an iron pot and stool nearby. Worktable and chairs are at left. Long table at center has cloth that hangs to floor; the table must be easy for Mother Goose to shake and move. Benches are on either side of it, and a high-backed chair is at the head, facing audience. Exit right leads to palace; exit left to outside.

Sound: Loud knocking on door; recorded violin music, as indicated in text.

THE RETURN OF BOBBY SHAFTO
(Play on pages 78–89.)

Characters: 5 male; 4 female.

Playing Time: 20 minutes.

Costumes: Bobby Shafto wears a velvet cape over nautical costume. He has on long white stockings and velvet cap. Later he removes shoes and stockings and replaces cape and cap with a ragged cloak and bandanna and puts on an eye patch. Sailors wear appropriate dress. Magnolia is dressed in white, with white parasol; Marigold is in yellow, and Morning Glory in purple. Each has a small purse containing letter. Maid Marjorie and Gardener wear peasant costumes. Lord Mayor wears an elaborate robe and hat.

Properties: Sea chest containing ragged cloak, bandanna, eye patch, seven bags of gold; letters; document for father; cart piled with fruits and vegetables.

Setting: A wharf in port of Florabella. Several packing cases, large enough to conceal Shafto and Sailors, are piled up at right. A small platform, representing a pier, is at left. Exits are at right and left.

Lighting: No special effects.

THE MOUSE THAT SOARED
(Play on pages 90–100.)

Characters: 4 male; 2 female; 12 male or female for other mice.

Playing Time: 20 minutes.

Costumes: Mice wear gray or brown outfits, with tights, sweaters, and mouse hats. Mamma Mouse may wear skirt. Bill and Jake wear everyday clothes. Thomas Cat wears a black cat outfit with a bell on a cord around his neck. Orvie re-enters at end wearing a space suit, which may be composed of dark tights, a heavy jacket and a helmet.

Properties: Blindfolds, cardboard carving knife, torn scrap of newspaper, transistor radio, pencil and sheets of paper, rhythm band instruments, including fiddle for Thomas Cat.

Setting: Merry Mouse Meadow. There is a tree upstage, and there may be a backdrop depicting a green landscape.

Lighting: No special effects.

Sound: Loud rumble like rocket taking off; static from radio.

THE GENTLE GIANT-KILLER
(Play on pages 101–115.)

Characters: 7 male; 10 female.

Playing Time: 25 minutes.

Costumes: Modern, everyday dress. Mr. Mason wears overalls.

Properties: Application form, pencil; attaché case containing pointed cap, sword, cloak, pair of fancy bedroom slippers; long-handled mop.

Setting: Before Rise: The Busy Bee Employment Agency. Two chairs and a desk with telephone and index card file are at one side of stage, in front of curtain. At Rise: Miss Goode's classroom has rows of desks. At one side is screen with names of parts of speech on large signs. Behind screen is a pile of straw, under which is envelope containing song sheets and note. A bookcase and other appropriate furnishings complete the setting. A door is right.

Lighting: No special effects.

Sound: Offstage roaring and banging, sounds of fight, as indicated in text.

SIMPLE SIMON'S REWARD
(Play on pages 116–131.)

Characters: 9 male; 7 female; 2 boys or girls for Children.

Playing Time: 20 minutes.

Costumes: Countess and Lord Scrubsville wear rich-looking costumes. Lord has a thick, bushy beard, in which earring is concealed. Countess wears one earring. Herald wears a uniform with rich trim. All other characters may wear traditional Mother Goose costumes: smocks or loose shirts for the men, and long dresses, aprons and kerchiefs or mobcaps for the women. All should have pockets for coins. Simple Simon carries a handkerchief in his pocket. If desired, everyday clothes may be worn in place of Mother Goose costumes.

Properties: Flyswatter, about 36 small pies or tarts (real or cardboard), cart, staff for Herald, handkerchief, coins, two "diamond" earrings, purse.

Setting: The road to fairground.

At center is an open booth, with many pies on counter. On it hangs a sign reading PIES FOR SALE. Two tables with chairs or benches are at each side of the booth. Exits are at left and right.

Lighting: No special effects.

SHIRLEY HOLMES AND THE FBI
(Play on pages 132–146.)

Characters: 5 female; 7 male; 3 male or female for Officers, announcer.

Playing Time: 20 minutes.

Costumes: All wear everyday clothes. Officers have on uniforms. Curly Smith and Baby Face Boyd have on sweat shirts with the letters SPHS on them; they wear half masks.

Properties: Two flashlights; large piece of paper; folder with papers; 5 mops; 5 pails; box holding pot and groceries; small stick with white flag; handcuffs.

Setting: An abandoned garage. Backdrop shows wall of gray cinder block. Door is at right. Workbench, center, is piled high with boxes, old radio, hot plate, etc. Cupboard is hidden in left corner, behind ladders, volleyball net, and canvas tarpaulin. Canvas bag, coffee can, and ledger book—all holding play money—are on shelf in cupboard. Tennis racket, baseball bat, canoe paddle, and other pieces of sports equipment are scattered around stage.

Sound: Police sirens; radio static.

VICKY GETS THE VOTE
(Play on pages 147–158.)

Characters: 8 male; 5 female.

Playing Time: 25 minutes.

Costumes: Everyday modern dress.

Properties: Ten flashlights; newspaper; paper and pen.

Setting: A comfortable living room furnished with a couch, chairs, tables, lamps, etc. A writing table or desk should be downstage, a telephone on a small table upstage.

Lighting: The lights go off and then come up as indicated in the text.

THE LITTLE NUT TREE
(Play on pages 159–169.)

Characters: 12 male; 9 female.

Playing Time: 15 minutes.

Costumes: Old-fashioned village costumes. Guide has sign on his hat and badge on his chest reading "Guide." Lord Mayor wears dignified black outfit. Princess Joanna, Heralds, Ladies-in-Waiting and Don Carlos wear regal, elaborate costumes. Princess wears a crimson dress and black wig.

Properties: Nut tree with silver nutmeg and golden pear (may be constructed from cardboard), stool or stepladder, bottles of polish, cloths, sprinkling cans, axe, trumpets, handkerchief.

Setting: The garden of the Poole family, in which the nut tree occupies a prominent place slightly right of center stage. Shrubbery, plants, etc., may be added to give the illusion of a garden. Exit at right leads to house; at left to street.

Sound: Trumpets. Music for "Little Nut Tree" may be found in many songbooks for children.

Lighting: No special effects.

THE GLASS SLIPPERS
(Play on pages 170–181.)

Characters: 7 male; 5 female; 8 male or female.

Playing Time: 20 minutes.

Costumes: Traditional fairy-tale costumes. Cobblers wear peasant shirts and trousers, with colorful sashes. Mother and Daughters wear elegant dresses. Cinderella wears ragged skirt and blouse. Old Woman wears dark dress, shawl, and scarf. Prince and Heralds wear court costumes; Prince wears crown. Customers wear dresses or shirts and trousers.

Properties: Shoes of all kinds, including gold slippers, silver slippers, bedroom slippers, and one pair of glass or plastic slippers; cobblers' tools, needle and thread, hammers, etc.; shoe boxes and bags; long table cover; bowl of soapsuds and long-stemmed pipe for blowing soap bubbles; cane.

Setting: The workshop of the Carefree Cobblers. At right is a long workbench with chairs behind it. At left is a small table with a chair at it. Down center is a display counter.

Lighting: No special effects.

THE MIRACULOUS TEA PARTY
(Play on pages 182–192.)

Characters: 8 female; 5 male.

Playing Time: 15 minutes.

Costumes: Everyday clothes for Mother and children. Minty wears her mother's hat, fur piece and high-heeled shoes, then slips into her own shoes later on. Book characters wear appropriate costumes.

Properties: Knitting; six books; plate of cookies; tray of lemonade and cookies; jump rope; baseball and bat; several hats for Bartholomew; bag of groceries; doll carriage.

Setting: Front lawn of the Stevens home. There is a large umbrella table right center, with six or seven chairs near it. Picket fence is down left. Exit right leads to house.

Lighting: Lights should go out for a few seconds at third clap of thunder.

Sound: Telephone ringing, thunder roll, as indicated in text.